Walter Bagehot

SOME ARTICLES ON THE DEPRECIATION OF SILVER AND ON TOPICS CONNECTED WITH IT

Elibron Classics
www.elibron.com

Elibron Classics series.

ISBN 1-4021-6288-X (paperback)
ISBN 1-4021-0507-X (hardcover)

This Elibron Classics Replica Edition is an unabridged facsimile of the edition published in 1877 by Henry S. King & Co., London.

THE DEPRECIATION OF SILVER.

RECENT WORKS BY THE SAME AUTHOR.

8vo. price 2s.

PARLIAMENTARY REFORM:

An Essay.

REPRINTED FROM "THE NATIONAL REVIEW."

8vo, price 2s.

HISTORY OF THE UNREFORMED PARLIAMENT, AND ITS LESSONS.

An Essay.

REPRINTED FROM "THE NATIONAL REVIEW."

CHAPMAN AND HALL, 193 PICCADILLY.

8vo, price 2s.

INTERNATIONAL COINAGE:

A Practical Plan for Assimilating the English and American Money, as a Step towards a Universal Money.

REPRINTED FROM "THE ECONOMIST."

LONGMANS AND CO., PATERNOSTER ROW.

SOME ARTICLES

ON THE

DEPRECIATION OF SILVER

AND ON

TOPICS CONNECTED WITH IT.

BY THE LATE

WALTER BAGEHOT.

Reprinted from "The Economist."

HENRY S. KING AND CO., LONDON.

1877.

LONDON: PRINTED AT THE EXETER HALL PRINTING WORKS,
18 EXETER STREET, STRAND, W.C.

PREFACE.

I VENTURE to bring together these articles on the recent Depreciation of Silver, and on the recent Exchanges with India, though I am well aware how incomplete a view they give of the complex subjects to which they relate, and how disagreeable to read a collection of such papers almost necessarily is. If I could, I would have rewritten the whole of them in a more systematic form. But I have no time or strength at my disposal for such a task, and I am obliged, therefore, to use this substitute. To elucidate some parts of the chain of reasoning, I have added the evidence which I gave on one or two points before Mr. Goschen's Committee on the Depreciation of Silver, last spring. But even so, there is much I should wish to say in addition, both in exposition and in defence of the opinions which I hold.

So far as the short experience which we have had goes, I think it confirms the view taken in these articles.

First, I consider that the rise in the price of silver from 47d. last summer to $55\frac{1}{4}$d. now, shows the preceding great fall from $54\frac{7}{8}$d. last February to be only a momentary accident in a new and weak market, and not the permanent effect of lasting causes.

Secondly, it has been proved that the demand for the countries which use silver as a currency is stimulated by its cheapness here and in America, and that this has carried off the late supply. China has taken the lead in so doing, mainly because she has had a better and readier means of export; but sooner or later, all other silver-moneyed countries will do so, according to their magnitude and opportunities.

And these are the two main propositions which I wish to establish.

If these are proved, the practical conclusion follows that it would be absurd to make any permanent changes in our Indian currency or taxation, while all the facts upon which such changes would be founded are changing so much and so rapidly. And though this conclusion does not need support, it is supported by our uncertainty as to the effect of the increased Home charges of our Indian Government—sometimes, for shortness, called the Indian "tribute"—which, in a way which I have tried to explain, complicates the whole subject.

The fertility of the new silver mines in America is not very elaborately examined in these articles, for even yet there are no sure data for us. But everything tends to show that the yield of these mines is likely to be far less than what was once thought, and the difficulty of obtaining exact data is an additional reason for being very slow to make any changes founded on an hypothesis as to the future price of silver. As yet no one can prove that the permanent value of silver—whether in relation to gold or in relation to commodities at large—will change so much as to render any alterations necessary.

[The Preface, as above written, was sent to the printers about the beginning of March. It is believed that Mr. Bagehot at one time contemplated making additions to it, but no memoranda have been left explanatory of his last intentions.

Economist Office, April, 1877.]

CONTENTS.

SOME ARTICLES

ON THE DEPRECIATION OF SILVER,

AND ON

TOPICS CONNECTED WITH IT.

I.

THE LOW VALUE OF SILVER, AND ITS EFFECT ON INDIA.

[From the "Economist" of February 5, 1876.]

When the great gold discoveries were made in Australia and California, most people expected that there would be a more or less rapid fall in the value of gold, as compared with silver. But, as a matter of fact, the effect has been the reverse. The value of silver as compared with gold was $59\frac{3}{4}$d. per oz., or as 1 to 15·7, in 1849; it now is $54\frac{3}{4}$d., or as 1 to 17·1. Not only what the best judges expected has not happened, but the very contrary of it has happened.

And this has not been the result of any collateral cause; it is the direct consequence of the gold discoveries themselves. The effect of these discoveries has been a great improvement in the currencies of the world, which, without them, would not have been possible. The countries of great commerce and large transactions require a more valuable medium of exchange, bulk for bulk, than countries of petty trade and minor transactions. The labour of paying £1,000,000 in sovereigns is only a tenth of that of paying it in rupees, and therefore where millions have to be paid sovereigns are a ten times better currency than rupees. Gold is much the best currency for rich nations of large trade; though silver does well enough, and is in some respects most suitable, for poor nations of little trade. But thirty years ago it would not have been possible for the nations of great commerce to have adopted this best currency. There would not have been gold enough obtainable. The supply from the mines was then barely sufficient to maintain the existing gold currencies; it would have been entirely insufficient for establishing new currencies on a large scale. No one then would ever have dreamed of proposing it. But, as we all know, Germany has just now tried the experiment on a great scale. She is buying gold, and selling off her silver. And in consequence silver is cheaper than it has ever been before.

Probably, if there were gold enough for all the world, it would be best that there should be only a single standard of value thoughout the world, and that one—gold. But this is impossible. Some have doubted whether there is gold enough even for the nations which now intend to use it; and there certainly is not enough for all the world. Happily, the

East has always been a country which had much silver, and for whose purposes silver was quite sufficient. The transactions of the East are small in comparison with those of the West, and therefore a bulky paying medium is not so inconvenient there as it would be here. Since economical history has been written silver has been always sent from Europe to China, India, and the richer parts of the East, and never more so than in our own time. The payments of England in silver to India during the cotton famine were probably the greatest cash payments ever made in so short a time by one country to another. There is therefore in the end a certain market for the silver displaced from Europe; it will ultimately go, as the rest has gone, to the East, where it is the ancient and the best-attainable paying medium.

But for the moment there is a difficulty in disposing of silver. There is no new sudden demand for it in the East. The case is not like that of the cotton famine. Then we had incurred a large debt to India, and we had to pay it in the only currency which she would take. We had to find an immense quantity of silver on a sudden, and France—owing to the peculiar operation of her double standard—found it for us. But now there is no such debt; the present problem is not to find the silver, but to find the use for the silver. And this is a slower process.

Sooner or later, however, the ordinary laws that govern foreign exchanges will do it for us. The consequence of the low value of silver is that the rate of exchange is now 1s. 9¼d. per rupee (or less), the lowest, or almost the lowest, ever known. And this operates as a direct discouragement to ship goods to India. These goods are paid for in rupees, and when the merchant wants to bring home those rupees to England he finds that they do not go so far as they used to do. He has to pay much more for every £1,000 bill on England, and this extra cost destroys or diminishes his profit.

Secondly, the same state of the exchanges is a direct premium on sending goods from India to England. £1,000 received for those goods here will go further in buying bills on India than it used to do; in plain English, it will lay down more rupees at Calcutta in the same time than formerly, and this increase is so much extra profit. By this combination, therefore, exports from India increasing on one hand, and imports into India diminishing on the other hand, before long a large void will be created, which this silver, set free from Germany, will have to fill. The process will take time, but the effect is inevitable. The tendency of this great import of silver into India will be of course to raise prices, but the degree in which it will have that effect will depend on the degree in which it is counteracted by the causes which have intercepted its effect before—the hoarding habits of the people; the use of silver in ornaments (the ornaments being a sort of reserve fund to be sold in difficulty); the greater extension of silver in rude districts, where barter is still much used; and the general increase of trade, which rising prices always tend to quicken and develop.

When this rise of prices has taken place, the encouragement to exports from and discouragement of imports into India will manifestly cease. The value of the rupee at Calcutta, as against bills on England, may remain as it is now; but the diminution of that value as compared with former times will be compensated by the greater number of rupees which the English exporter to India obtains for the goods which he sells there. The value of the £1,000 in London in purchasing bills payable on India in rupees may be as unusually great as now, if we compare it with the past, but there will be a corresponding difficulty in obtaining the £1,000 in London. The merchant in India will have to pay more for the goods which he sends to London, and in the end this loss will be equal to the other gain.

If new silver should still continue to come into the market the same process must go on. The first step must be incessantly repeated. The value of the rupee must fall as against sterling money; instead of being 1s. 9d., it may fall to 1s. 6d. And then, *mutatis mutandis*, what we have just described as happening will happen again.

The effect, therefore, of the fall in the value of silver on the trade of India will be temporary only, but its effect on the financial position of the Indian Government will continue as long as the fall lasts. The Indian revenue is received in silver, and, therefore, the less far silver goes in buying, the poorer will the Indian Government be. And this is of more instant importance to the Indian Government than almost any other, because its foreign payments exceed those of most Governments, and those payments are made in gold. It has to pay interest in gold on a very large debt in England, to pay home salaries, maintain home depôts, and buy English goods and stores all in gold; and the less valuable silver is in comparison with gold, the less effectual for these necessary purposes will the Indian revenue be.

On one species of its debt the Indian Government will, indeed, not lose. The interest upon rupee paper is payable in rupees in Calcutta, and therefore the diminution in the value of the rupee is a loss to the creditor who receives, and not to the Government which pays.

How long the fall in the value of silver will continue no one can say. In the last resort, and taking great intervals of time into the reckoning, the relative value of gold and silver will be determined by their cost of production; but in the case of articles so durable, and so liable to be affected by political events like changes in coinage, it is difficult to say how long an average must be taken in order to exhibit distinctly this final result.

II.

THE REMEDIES FOR THE FALL IN SILVER.

[From the "Economist" of March 4, 1876.]

The fall in the value of silver, of which we spoke weeks since, and which has attracted so much attention, proceeds from three causes. First, the actual increase of the production of silver, especially in America, the extent of which is very considerable, as will be seen by the figures we give below; secondly, the amount of silver which has been set free by the German coinage operations, and has been sold here and elsewhere; and, lastly, the perturbed state of men's minds, which is consequent on these events. So large an increase of the supply makes dealers fear a still larger further increase, and therefore they do not wish to buy, and do not care to hold. When markets are in this temper speculations are for the fall, and not for the rise, and therefore there is just now a disposision to "bear" silver and to force its price down. Over and above the proper effect of the causes in operation, there is an additional effect consequent on apprehensive opinion.

The evils of the fall thus caused are two, and both of great importance. First, our English exporters to India and the East find their profits diminished or changed into a loss. They are paid in silver, which is the currency of those countries, but when they bring that silver home and turn it into gold, which is our currency, they find it is not worth nearly so much as it used to be, and this diminution is so much loss to them. In the presence of stagnant and unprofitable trade, such a sudden change for the worse is not easily borne, and its effect, as is usual in such cases, will be propagated through other trades. Secondly, the Indian revenue is received in silver, and the Indian Government, which has to send some £15,000,000 home annually, for interest on its debt and other purposes, finds, in the same way, that the drafts from England on India, by which the remittance is effected, will not go as far as they used to do.

In the end, as we before showed, this fall in silver will work its own cure. Every country is bound to take any quantity of its own money in payment for debts due to it. As has been just explained, imports *into* India are no longer profitable; and by the converse operation of the same causes, exports *from* India have become more profitable than usual. The silver price of Indian commodities in India has not as yet risen much, though silver has fallen here as compared with gold, and there is, therefore, more profit than there was in exporting them. They can be bought with the same sum in silver, and that silver can be obtained more easily. The balance of trade will thus be, as the old writers used to count, constantly very favourable to India; silver will be necessarily sent thither, and the prices there will rise. As far as commerce is concerned, at a certain time everything will be as it was before the fall began. The imports into India will be as profitable as before, because the silver prices in India will have risen as much as silver has fallen in relation to gold, and the exports from India for the same reason, turned the other way, will not be more profitable than usual. The equation of trade, as theoretical writers term it, will be as before. And if the Indian Government were like most Governments, its position also would not be altered. As its taxes were paid in a medium of less value as compared with commodities, it must raise its taxes by an equivalent amount. But, unhappily, the position of the Indian Government is peculiar. The best portion of its revenue is derived from rent, and not from taxation, and that rent is fixed for stated periods—usually thirty years—in advance. On the £21,000,000 which the Indian Government thus receives there will be a loss, which it will have to make good by some financial expedient; and, as we well know, financial expedients are not so easy in India as they are in England. Still, such is the natural effect of these economical causes, and such the ultimate cure for the evils which are due to them.

As usual, however, other cures are suggested which, it is said, will be less painful and quicker—one is that the Indian Government should demonetise silver, as the Germans have been doing, and adopt a gold standard. But in this case the remedy would be worse than the disease. We all know what the Germans have had to do, and how painful its effect upon us has been. They have had to buy gold to substitute for that silver, and the result has been an unusual disturbance of the London market, with sometimes very high rates of discount; nor is the operation yet complete. But the effect of a similar operation in India upon us would be altogether greater and more disturbing, because the Indian silver currency is so very much greater than the German. To get gold enough to supply the place of all this silver the Indian Government would have to buy constantly all the supplies from the gold mines for years, and so straighten incalculably the growing money markets of the world. And then what is the Indian Government to do with the silver? The sales of the German Government have greatly helped to send the price down already; the Indian sales would be on a much greater scale, and would come upon the market just when the supplies from the new American mines were arriving also. So much silver could scarcely be sold at all; the best result to the Indian Government from this expedient would be far worse than anything which it is enduring now by letting things take their course—besides the disturbance to the London and other money markets.

Secondly, it is suggested that the German Government should not sell any more silver, and so not reduce the price. But we may be sure that the German Government will be guided, as in such a case it ought to be, by a regard to its own interest. When it thinks it best to sell it will sell. Like any other holder of silver, it loses much interest by keeping very large sums; and looking to the possible magnitude of the American supply, it will probably not wish to incur for certain that great present loss at the risk also of a still further loss by depreciation. We cannot control the German Government; it will act for its own interest, and it is best that it should.

Thirdly, it is said that our Government should cease to draw bills on India. And our Government is quite right in doing so at the present moment. There is, as we said before, at present in our judgment an apprehensive opinion which exaggerates the effect of the real causes at work—and also, as we are inclined to believe, speculation acting on and aggravating that opinion. In such a state of the market the Indian Government is quite right in doing as little as it can, and it would do ill to hurry to incur a loss which may be saved. But sooner or later it must bring the necessary sums home from India, and must bear whatever loss accompanies its so doing.

Fourthly, it is suggested by M. Cernuschi, the eminent French economist, that England, which was the first country to adopt the single gold standard, should take the initiative in abandoning it; that it should give up the present silver-token currency, and instead, "coin pounds sterling of silver in pieces of four shillings, and, concurrently with gold, put them into circulation." But the English Government and nation will not easily be persuaded to abandon the monetary policy which they invented, and which on the whole has been so successful, just when all other nations are adopting it. The loss of profit on our present gold circulation, the cost of selling it and substituting a silver currency, are in themselves very considerable objections. It would take a very much greater evil than we, or than India, now feel from the present depreciation of silver, to outweigh them. The moment, too, would seem to the practical English sense most ill-chosen to choose to coin silver as a concurrent medium with gold, and therefore necessarily in a fixed relation with gold, just when silver is falling in value, and when we are not sure what its relation to gold will be. Monsieur Cernuschi speaks of the "universality of the 15½." "Since 1803," he says, "the silver franc has weighed 15½ francs of gold, and the silver marc now weighs 15½ marcs of gold," and he would have us coin on this assumption, and in this proportion. But the actual question is whether, in the face of the new and cheap supplies now brought from the American mines, this proportion can be maintained. Even if the best theoretical arguments could be urged for this proposal, it would for many years seem a paradox to our straightforward English minds, and they would be very slow to decide on adopting it.

But we think the theoretical argument is the other way, that it is in favour of our present English coinage, and not of M. Cernuschi's proposed substitute. We differ from him on a fundamental point of principle. He says that "the cost of production does not determine the value of gold and silver. That value is determined by two elements—the employment and the quantity." But we say, on the other hand, that the value of gold and silver is determined by their cost of production, just like that of all other things; that in their case—as in all other cases—what is more cheaply produced than usual will be more plentifully produced than usual, and that the purchasing power in consequence will be no doubt less. Being durable articles, gold and silver are articles stable in general, though not always, in value, as compared with other things, and a change in their cost of production does not so soon affect their value as a corresponding change in the cost of other commodities affects theirs. But the delay does not impair the principle; in the end, its effects will come.

The same causes which regulate the value of gold and silver as respects other things determine, as we believe, their value relatively to each other, and, therefore, as the circumstances of production of both are constantly changing, it is contrary to principle to make, or attempt to make by law, a fixed equation between them. So far, therefore, from M. Cernuschi's proposal being recommended by abstract argument, we think such argument forbids it, as well as its unlikely look, which, for a long time, will have as much or more effect on most English minds than any argument.

Lastly, M. Cernuschi recommends that Germany and Holland, which are in the course of demonetising their silver, though at very different stages, should carefully consider before they go any further. And we do not feel able to say what effect this present fall in the price of silver should have on their present plans. All changes in currency are delicate things, and we quite admit—indeed, we have often before maintained—that this is a particularly delicate one.

But these are considerations for foreign Governments only. For our own Government and that of British India, we believe that there is no other policy possible except to leave the ordinary economical causes to operate—to suffer the present evil, and to await the ultimate cure.

Estimate of Silver Product of the United States (converting the Dollars into Sterling at 4s. each).

	£
From 1849 to 1858, £10,000 per annum	100,000
1859	20,000
1860	30,000
1861	400,000
1862	900,000
1863	1,700,000
1864	2,200,000
1865	2,250,000
1866	2,000,000
1867	2,700,000
1868	2,400,000
1869	2,400,000
1870	3,200,000
1871	4,600,000
1872	5,750,000
1873	7,150,000
1874 (about)	7,000,000

The above figures are taken from the Reports of the United States Director of the Mint.

III.

FURTHER SUGGESTIONS ON THE FALL IN SILVER.

[From the "Economist" of March 11, 1876.]

The grave difficulties which the Indian Government finds in consequence of the fall in silver, and the much graver ones which it has to apprehend if that fall goes further and further, have naturally led to various suggestions, two of which are important enough to deserve notice. First, it has been suggested that the Indian Government should compel the ryots to pay the land-revenue in gold at a fixed rate of exchange, say, 10 rupees to the sovereign, and it has been thought we shall so obtain most of the advantages of the demonetisation of silver without any of the disadvantages. But this we believe to be a mistake. The measure, in the first place, would augment the depreciation of silver as compared with gold. Silver is at present the medium in which the land-revenue is paid; if it is excluded from that class of payments and gold substituted, the rejected metal will fall and the adopted one rise in comparative value. The ryot who has silver ready to pay his land-tax, finding that silver useless, must exchange it for gold, and an incessant series of such transactions would augment the depreciation which is complained of.

Secondly, the ryot would complain, and justly, of breach of contract. The Government agreed with him to take so much silver for so many years, but now, in effect, it says it must have so much more silver. Suppose the silver rupee were only equal to 1s. 8d. in gold, and you make him find gold at 2s. a rupee; this is equal to an addition of one-sixth to his taxation, and this will be a great hardship. If, indeed, the prices which the ryot gets for his commodities in silver had risen, he would be benefited as much as he lost, but as yet this is not so. The effect upon the relation of silver to gold has been much quicker than that upon the silver prices of miscellaneous commodities, and it would be a severe tyranny and real breach of faith, to increase the stated land-tax upon the ryot when his means of paying that tax had not been augmented.

Thirdly, the Indian creditors of the Government, who are paid in silver, would say that their contract ought to be put on the same footing as the ryot's contract; that as he is to pay in gold, at a fixed rate, so ought they to be paid. And their case will be stronger, because, as we have seen, the depreciation of silver will be increased by this action of the Government; and, therefore, its creditors may justly claim not to suffer by that which is, in part, at least, the act of their own debtor.

Fourthly, the officials of the Indian Government will at once say that they ought to be paid in gold too, at a fixed rate. And there would be a real claim to it as far as the English officials are concerned, for they are in much the same position as the Government; they have to make large remittances to England for the investments of their savings, and often for the maintenance of their families. The prospect of making these savings has very much induced them to go to India, and, therefore, it would be unfair by any act of Government materially to lessen their power of making them.

Other objections might be urged, but these are, we think, enough to show that the plan cannot be adopted.

The second scheme is even less plausible; indeed, we notice it rather because it has been spoken of in the market than for any merit it has. It is that the English Government should abstain from drawing on India, and should negotiate a loan in London. But this would only augment the evil, for the interest on the new loan would have to be paid in gold, and would be so much more if the gold was to be bought by the Indian Government in depreciated silver.

In so far as the evil is real there is, as we before showed, nothing to be done, except to endure the evil for the present, and to have confidence that the slow action of economical causes will in the end cure it. How far the present apprehensions are well grounded, and in what proportion on the contrary exaggerated, it would be as yet very premature to give an opinion.

IV.

THE EFFECTS OF THE RESUMPTION OF SPECIE PAYMENTS IN FRANCE ON THE PRICE OF SILVER.

[From the "Economist" of March 18, 1876.]

The increased supply of silver from the American mines, the amount of it thrown on the market by the coinage operations of Germany, and the consequent fall in its value as compared with gold, have all been much discussed; but there is another event which will have a great effect on the matter, and which must sooner or later happen, that has not received at all equal attention, viz., the resumption of specie payments by the Bank of France. The result of this, unless a change in the French coinage law is made, will be, we think, considerably to raise the price of silver as compared with gold, just as the result of the other causes which have been mentioned has been considerably to lower it.

Our older readers, and those of our younger ones who have followed the history of the London money market, will remember the exchange in 1860 of £2,000,000 of silver by the Bank of France for £2,000,000 of gold with the Bank of England, and the interest which it excited. We then explained what had happened, and the reason for it;—

"Why, then, do the Bank of France desire this arrangement? According to their own views, it was from no uneasiness as to their position. Notwithstanding the diminution in their reserve of bullion, they believe that they need feel no anxiety. By their last return their liabilities were:—

Notes in circulation...	£30,296,520
Deposits, &c.	15,176,102
Total	£45,472,622

and their reserve was more than £17,000,000, and they consider that this is amply sufficient.

"The difficulty of the Bank of France, it is said, is not the amount of bullion they hold, but the nature of that bullion. In their seventeen millions, the proportions are in round numbers:—

Gold	£4,000,000
Silver	13,000,000
Total	£17,000,000

And under the French currency laws this is not satisfactory. The Bank of France, for very sufficient reasons, prefer discharging their liabilities in gold instead of in silver. If they were to pay a noteholder £1,000 in silver, he could immediately sell the silver in the market for gold, and gain a substantial premium by the transaction. Accordingly the managers of the Bank of France apprehend that if they began to discharge their liabilities in silver, there would be a run upon them immediately for the sake of this premium. 'If every noteholder knew that he could obtain an appreciable per-centage on his note by getting it changed, depend on it,' they say, 'he will get it changed. The same causes which have drained the rest of France of silver (except for the smallest purposes, and of insufficient quantities even for those purposes) would begin to act upon us also; in a short time we should be drained of the whole of our thirteen millions of silver.' And this, they say, is the reason for their proposing this anomalous arrangement to the Directors of the Bank of England.

"One remark must occur to every one when he hears this reasoning. It is the remark that no bank ever ought to be in this position. There must be some fault somewhere; there must either be bad management or bad legislation; there must be some peculiar error, or there could hardly be so peculiar a perplexity. For what is the allegation? The Bank of France say we have a large reserve, but it is not the kind of reserve we want. It is in the wrong metal; it is not gold, but silver. The alternative is irresistible that either the Directors of the Bank have themselves made an error in hoarding a reserve in the wrong metal, or that circumstances beyond their power have forced upon them a hoard which they find they cannot use. They have a useless reserve, they themselves tell us; either, therefore, they have voluntarily selected it—in which case they are to blame; or it has, by an unfortunate necessity, been forced upon them—in which case they are not to blame.

"Nor is this the only remark which must immediately be made. There is another very obvious but very important one. This useless reserve is a misfortune, not to the Bank of France only, not to the French only, but to us also, to Europe, and to the whole monetary world. We have thirteen millions sterling thus locked away in a great banking establishment, which does not dare to use any part of that sum, for fear it may be deprived of all of it; and we have all been sufferers in consequence. The French demand for gold has been disturbing us for several weeks.

"In truth the entire difficulty is caused by the French currency laws. There has been a question whether there is a double standard of value in France, and we will not, therefore, use the phrase, but there is indisputably a *double paying medium.* Both gold and silver circulate in France; both are legal tenders to any amount; and there is a fixed relation between them. A certain quantity of silver by law will pay a debt of 1,000 francs, and a certain quantity of gold will pay it also. One effect of this twofold currency has been often pointed out. The metal which is relatively depreciated will come into exclusive use; people will pay their debts in the least valuable metal, not in the most valuable; in the medium which they can obtain *most* easily, not in the medium which they obtain *less* easily. But we have now to remark a different effect. *Some* of the holders of the more valuable metal may be in a difficulty. If they are bound to pay either the less or the more valuable metal to their creditors, and they have not the former, they must use the latter. In consequence, in a country where two metals are a paying medium, those bankers who store up either metal for the necessary purposes of their business run a great risk.

If it increases in value, there may be a run upon them, not because their credit is impaired, but because the metal they have chosen is desired."*

And the same cause will act on the Bank of France as soon as it resumes specie payments. The Bank of France holds now over £70,000,000 in the precious metals, and it is known that gold preponderates largely. Roughly, it is said that the proportions are—

Gold	£50,000,000
Silver	20,000,000
Total	£70,000,000

And here, just as in 1860, the principal component in the reserve is the comparatively *ap*preciated metal. The metals have, indeed, changed places; in 1860 the metal which had augmented in value was silver; now the metal which has increased in value is gold. But the position of the Bank of France is for the purpose now in hand identical. It now holds an enormous amount of gold, which it would be dangerous to pay away; just as in 1860 it held a much smaller, though still considerable, amount of silver, to pay away which would have been equally dangerous.

The basis of the difficulty is that the French Mint coins the two metals thus—

One kilogramme weight of gold	3,100 francs.
" " " silver... ...	200 "

— or in the proportion of $15\frac{1}{2}$. But this is not the real proportion of the market value. $15\frac{1}{2}$ is equivalent to about $60\frac{1}{4}$d. for an ounce of silver, whereas the market price is now $54\frac{1}{4}$d. The law having fixed

* See ECONOMIST, November 24, 1860, pp. 1301-2.

an equation, bankers will always be in difficulty when the facts with which they must deal do not correspond to that equation.

Of course, as long as the Bank of France suspends specie payments it does not feel this difficulty. If we may be permitted to say so, it is on a lower level altogether. It is not perplexed by the possibility of having to pay in the appreciated metal, for it does not, except in minor sums and when it chooses, pay in any metal. But as soon as the Bank of France performs its legal obligations, the problem which the defective currency system of France sets before it must be solved. There is, indeed, one obvious mode of solving it. There is something very singular in a difficulty which is caused by holding a commodity which has enhanced in value. The obvious remedy is to sell it in the market, and to obtain the advantage of that value. If the Bank of France could sell its gold for silver at the present price, it would get a large profit; it would have done a capital bullion transaction on a magnificent scale, and the shareholders would be large gainers in consequence. In 1860, the Emperor Napoleon, to whom the accounts of the Bank of France were then constantly submitted, would not permit this natural remedy to be tried, and, therefore, the Bank of France had to forego the profit, and to change away the dearer metal with the Bank of England. But now there can be no choice; the sums to be dealt with are so large that no such palliative by exchange can be thought of. If cash payments are to be resumed in France, large sales of gold for silver must precede and accompany the resumption.

And the effect of such sales will, of course, be to raise the price of silver as compared with gold. The circumstances of the Bank of France will make the possession of much silver constantly essential to it, and the effect of this new large demand will be a rise of price.

The only alternative is the demonetisation of silver, and if this could be effected, it would give France a currency much better than the present one, according to our notions. The *bi*-metallic system is, we think, condemned by the very discussion in which we are engaged, for the perplexities which that system entails on the Bank of France are the evils of which we are seeking the remedy. But it may be doubted whether France is now prepared to abandon this system. It would be a very costly operation. The amount of five-franc pieces hoarded in France is probably very large, and if they are to be demonetised, gold must be substituted for them, which, as the example of Germany shows us, is no easy thing to do. Moreover, till 1880, France is bound by a monetary convention with Italy, Switzerland, and Belgium, and can only change as they like. Even after 1880, France would not like to abandon the "Latin Union," as it is called, which is economically convenient—which is her creation, for it is an adoption of the money she desired, and in which she takes a political pride. Probably, if silver is demonetised at all, it will be so at once, not only in France, but in all those other States, which will be difficult to arrange, and costly to effect. And it will not have the united support of theoretical opinion, for many Continental — and especially

French—economists adhere to the two-metal plan. And even strong opponents of that plan (like ourselves) may well doubt whether this is the time to abandon it. The Governments who do so undertake, in fact, to substitute gold for silver, and just now they have unusual difficulty in getting the gold, and in disposing of the silver. Germany is just making the substitution, and it is obviously an operation in which many great nations should not engage contemporaneously. An interval ought rather to be left after the completion of the operation by one before another begins.

It is true that the demonetisation will be facilitated by the clauses in the agreement of the Latin Union, which limit the number of silver pieces less than five-francs to be coined by each State in the union, and which limit the amount for which such subordinate pieces are legal tender. These pieces might, therefore, still be left to circulate as token-money. But, nevertheless, the change, especially in so many States at once, would be a heavy task to accomplish, and not one which it would be easy to get undertaken. And failing this, there is no remedy, except the sale of gold for silver by the Bank of France, of which we have spoken, so soon as a return to specie payments is determined on.

It may, indeed, be suggested that the Bank of France need not return to specie payments at all. But we do not believe that those who have managed her affairs so admirably during the last few years will even consider that alternative. As bankers who have promised to pay on demand, they must wish to maintain their credit by so paying. And Paris can never again be the exchange centre for Europe which it used to be, and which many concurring circumstances render it convenient for it to be, while bills on Paris are paid in a purely local medium like the paper of the Bank of France, and not in the precious metals, which are the money of all the world.

Sooner or later, therefore, we have no doubt that the Bank of France will resume specie payments, and then, unless the fundamental basis of the French currency law shall have been first changed, there will be a very material rise in the value of silver as compared with gold.

V.

THE EFFECT OF A DEPRECIATION OF SILVER ON OUR FOREIGN, AND ESPECIALLY ON OUR EASTERN TRADE.

[FROM THE "ECONOMIST" OF MAY 6, 1876.]

THAT the depreciation of silver as compared with gold, which has already begun, and of which we cannot yet predict the final amount, is unfavourable to the Indian Government, is plain. That Government receives a revenue in silver which it cannot easily augment, and it has to find annually, for the interest on its Debt and for home expenses, a large sum of gold in London. Whatever lessens the value of silver as compared with gold is therefore very disadvantageous to it. And whatever does so is also detrimental to the holders of Indian or other securities of which the interest is paid in silver. But it is only States or persons in this position—that is, those in receipt of a more or less fixed sum in silver—who will permanently be affected by it. After the depreciation of silver has attained its limit trade will be exactly where it is now, and though during the process there will be much unsatisfactory uncertainty in the trades with the countries whose prices are in silver, and though in some parts our trade will probably suffer, yet other parts will as probably be benefited;

and therefore this change, though like all changes in the value of a currency, a troublesome burthen, is, nevertheless, not an evil of the first magnitude, or at all likely to produce the disastrous effects, on English commerce especially, which we sometimes see expected from it.

We must remember that silver is still practically the main currency of a very large part of the world. The whole of the East uses it, not indeed to the entire exclusion of gold, but still much more than gold. It suits the minuteness of the payments which in Oriental countries, and in all countries in which there is no credit, of necessity make up almost the whole of the daily transactions which carry on common life, and for which the smallest gold coin that can be safely and economically used is very many times too great. Over the vast area of the backward pale of the world an incalculable quantity of silver is now scattered, doing the work of daily life, and doing it almost to the exclusion of all other currencies. And we must remember, too, that with this currency, as with all others, the efficiency depends on the value. The more things a rupee exchanges for, the fewer rupees will be necessary to do the work of India. A change of 10 per cent. in the purchasing power of silver would make 10 per cent. more silver necessary in each of these countries; and though we do not know what 10 per cent. would amount to, because we really cannot tell even approximately the quantity of silver circulating in those countries, yet we see that it must amount to something very large, for that present circulation must be reckoned by hnndreds of millions. To make a permanent change even of small amount in the purchasing power of silver throughout the world is a most costly matter, requiring much time. No commodity is of so stable a value as a great deal of money diffused over many countries, because as soon as you diminish that value even a little, you augment the quantity required indefinitely. In this case, far more than in any other, an addition to the supply of itself generates an addition to the demand.

And a depreciation of such money is necessarily diffused with more or less rapidity through the various nations who use it. A local congestion, so to speak, is impossible. The laws which distribute the precious metals over the world will gradually lessen the value in all of them, if it is greatly and suddenly lowered in any one. There is a steady tendency to take such a commodity from the country where its purchasing power is small to those in which its purchasing power is great, and in that way this power settles in all countries at its level.

Such a change in the value of a metallic money will even generate a new trade between countries which had none before. The discovery of gold in Australia and California gave those countries a buying power which created a great direct commerce with them; the nations from whom they bought obtained a buying power too; so on with those from whom they bought; and so an unprecedented accession to the previous trade of the world.

It would be absurd to expect any results of similar or approaching magnitude from the new silver mines in America, even were their magnitude and fertility many times greater than even the most sanguine computers make them. But the same cardinal principles will govern this smaller case which we have seen govern the greater. The silver prices of all articles must gradually and slowly be raised all through the silver countries; and the rise will be effected the most quickly in those countries which have most share in the commerce of the world, and which export and import most. Take the case of India at this time. The depreciation of silver in London is an encouragement to English capitalists to buy commodities—jute, cotton, indigo, or whatever it may be—in India. Such commodities are sold in rupees, that is, in silver, in the Calcutta market. Now, an English capitalist must first buy his rupees—for this is the real result of the more complex exchange transactions — before he can obtain these commodities. The cheaper, therefore, he can buy such rupees the better his operation. Supposing an order to buy at a given hour in the Calcutta market to yield neither profit nor loss when rupees were at 2s., it might yield a good profit if the rupee fell to 1s. 8d., because then the gold of the English capitalist would go so much further in the purchase of them.

The very contrary arises in the case of English exports to India. The English exporter of these is paid in rupees at Calcutta or Bombay, and these rupees, when he brings them home to London, are worth (say) a sixth less than they used to be; and, therefore, he has a steady and certain motive not to export as much as he used to do. And the sure result of these two changes, of the encouragement of exports from India and of the discouragement of imports into India, is a flow of silver from hence thither, which must ultimately raise the general standard of prices there.

It may be objected that this rise of prices will be an evil to India—will throw it out of the world's market; that Indian cotton, for example, which has thus risen in price, will not be able to compete with American cotton, of which the price will be unaltered. But this objection is fallacious; all which the rise of prices will effect will be to withdraw the exceptional encouragement which, as we have just explained, the present state of things gives to the export of Indian cotton. When silver has settled to its new level of value all trade, whether of export to, or import from India, will go on as it did when it was at its old value. Take the case of the English importer from India, silver having fallen (say) 15 per cent. In its relation to gold, he will get 15 per cent. more rupees than he used to do for his gold, but when he goes into the Calcutta market, he will find that these rupees will only purchase an equal per-centage less; his gold will be neither more nor less efficient than at first, and therefore he will neither be encouraged to buy nor discouraged from buying. Conversely, the English exporter to India will not be able to get as much for the rupees for which he sells his goods, when he brings those rupees home here; but on the other hand, he will have, to a corresponding extent, more rupees, and therefore the final outcome of his trade will not be altered.

No doubt it is true that during the process of depreciation our general export trade to some countries will be under a disadvantage. We shall export to them silver instead of goods; but on the other hand, certain other branches of our foreign trade will be augmented. The silver which we send to India we shall have sent to us from America, and we shall have to pay for it. And we shall doubtless pay for it in the same way that we pay America for the rest of the commodities which she sends us. Our present direct trade with America stands thus:—

Export from America to England (1874)	...	£73,897,000
„ England to America „	...	32,238,000
Balance in favour of America ...	...	£41,659,000

And against this balance America draws drafts to pay for what she buys in India, in China, or in France, and all over the world. The trade is what is called a triangular trade, because the debt due to one nation is paid for, not by the nation which owes it, but by some other nation or nations which are in debt to that nation. The more, therefore, we augment our American trade, the more we shall have to export in goods, not indeed wholly, or probably principally, to America itself, but to other countries to which she is in debt. And as America always buys more in the East than she sells there, curiously enough one of the trades which will most likely be thus stimulated is the trade with the East, which from the first operation of the new cause—by the substitution of silver for goods in our direct trade—has been discouraged and depressed.

The same fact may be put in another way. The United States have acquired by the extraordinary productiveness of their new mines of silver an augmented purchasing power in the markets of the world. The increase of power they use in buying the commodities which they wish for in the East and throughout the world. But partly owing to her protective system, and partly in consequence of natural causes, America has no direct communication with the countries which produce those goods; she therefore sends the silver to England, and England acts for her as a produce-broker on a vast scale —both sends on the silver to the countries which want it, and pays, indirectly, for what she buys to the countries she buys from. That we are able so to pay is one of the many instances in which, in trade, most is given to those who already have most. Our export trade is so much greater and so much more easily augmented than that of any other country, because we are able to settle any debt in commodities far better than any other nation. If the United States buy of nation B, B is more likely to want something of England than of any one else, or if, instead, B buys of C, C is so likely, and so on through the alphabet, till at last you come to England. Our predominant international trade gives us, in a business such as this, an assured pre-eminence.

This is one compensation for any evil to our present export trade, which may be caused by a change in the value of silver; and another is that a part of our import trade will, as we have seen, be benefited by the same cause; which must either cause—according to circumstances—increased profits to our traders, or diminished prices to our consumers; and either way, be a gain.

In thus writing, we have been content to assume

that the American production of new silver will be on the largest scale which has ever been alleged, because we wanted to show how large the area of silver-using countries is; how slow, in consequence, will be the process of depreciation; how much of benefit, as well as of loss, there is to our trade while the process is going on; and how much commerce will return to its antecedent state when the change has run its course, and the depreciation has terminated.

VI.

THE EXTREME FALL IN SILVER, AND THE HASTY REMEDIES PROPOSED.

[From the "Economist" of July 8, 1876.]

The report of Mr. Goschen's Committee on the depreciation of silver has been laid on the table, and will doubtless appear immediately. And it is understood to contain a most full analysis of all the causes which have combined to produce this perplexing event. But in the meantime the fall of the rupee to 1s. 6½d. at the last bidding for Council bills, and of silver to 47d. per oz., have naturally caused the suggestion in various quarters of various hasty remedies, which can be discussed before we get the report, because by the terms of their reference the Committee were debarred from considering remedies, and told to confine themselves to causes.

The main evils of this depreciation are two. First, and most important, that the Government of India receives the whole of its revenue in silver—partly in land-rents fixed for considerable periods, and partly in taxes which it is difficult to increase, and that this Government has also of necessity to find in London a very large amount in gold annually; so that they lose a sum which, taking the rupee at 1s. 8d., Sir William Muir, the Indian Finance Minister, estimated to be of most serious magnitude, and which, now that the rupee has fallen to 1s. 6½d., will be considerably more. So grave a misfortune has seldom happened to any Government so suddenly and so completely from causes out of its control. Secondly, all private persons, such as the holders of rupee paper, who have to receive fixed sums in silver, lose, as is usual when a currency becomes depreciated. Debtors gain and creditors lose in this instance, as in all similar ones. The great peculiarity of the case is the position of the Indian Government, which has so great a burden so rapidly thrown upon it, and is so little able by additional taxation with equal rapidity to find means to bear it.

The remedies suggested are, first, that the Government of India should demonetise silver and substitute gold. But those who make this proposal cannot have considered what in practice it would involve. A Government which abolishes an old money must find a new one. It could not say, "Our law up to the present time has made the silver rupee legal tender, but we now change that, and make a gold coin legal tender, which gold coin you, our subjects, must find for yourselves." If the Indian Government did so, the losses to its subjects would be enormous. Every holder of the old coinage who wanted to pay a debt would have to sell silver, which is so rapidly going down, and buy gold, which in comparison is rapidly rising, and the loss would be severe. The only way in which such an operation can be effected, is that which the German Government has lately adopted. That Government bought and found the gold which was to form the new currency, and in so far as the operation is complete, has exchanged it for the old one. But no one could now propose this to the Indian Government as a means of relieving itself from financial difficulty, for the cost which it would entail would be enormous. Even with all their resources, they would have great difficulty in getting the immense sum required in gold, and they would hardly be able to sell the silver at any price. The present position of the Indian Exchequer is not good, but it is beyond comparison better than it would be if this expedient were tried.

Secondly, it is suggested that we should adopt a double standard for India both of gold and silver. But this does not meet the difficulty. The effect of a double standard is, at every change in the relative value of the two metals, to fill the country with the metal which is falling. France, in this way, was during the cotton famine cleared of a large part of her silver, and gold was substituted for it. Bullion dealers sent the gold to buy the silver, and made a profit of the transaction. The "bad money" always drives out the "good;" and the Indian Exchequer would gain nothing. The essence of the "double standard" is to create two legal tenders, and give the debtor the choice of paying in which he likes. The Indian ryot would, of course, pay in silver, just as now, and the land revenue would be as much impaired for the purposes for which it is wanted, by the depreciation of silver as it is at present.

Thirdly, it is suggested that the Indian Government should cease to coin rupees, and that, in consequence, though the value of uncoined silver fell, that of the coin would not fall—its supply being restricted. But the effect of such a measure would be to reduce the price of silver far below even its present low amount, because it would stop the greatest natural demand for it, by stopping additions to the silver currency of India. And then the difference in value between the rupee as a coin and the same quantity of the uncoined silver, would be much greater than it would be possible to maintain. Good rupees would be a profitable article of manufacture, and would be imported largely from abroad and illicitly manufactured in India. Many Governments have tried a similar expedient, and have, in the end, always been beaten, and obliged to keep the price of their legal tender-coin near to the cost at which it can be produced. But in no case would the failure be so great as in that of India, because in none has the experiment ever been tried on a coin so important, and of so vast a circulation as the rupee.

The effect also would be that the difficulty of disposing of silver in London, and the consequent lowness of the price, would become worse and worse. The natural cure for the depreciation of silver is that it should be diffused over the globe, and especially over the immense area in the East, and elsewhere, which has a silver currency. If silver is depreciated 2 per cent. in all countries where it is the sole or main currency, 2 per cent. more silver must be required, and as the amount of silver in circulation in such countries is enormous, 2 per cent. upon it would be a very great demand, and take out of this market a very large quantity of silver. As we have shown on a former occasion,* the laws of trade will infallibly create this demand, though this action is necessarily slow. But the effect of not coining the rupee, in so far as it is successful, would be to suspend them altogether, as far as India is concerned, because it is only by arresting the reduction in the exchange value of the rupee that this step can help the Indian Government, and that reduction is the means by which, as we showed, the new course of trade is created, and the increased quantity of rupees required to do the work of Indian currency after that reduction constitutes the new demand for silver and the new use of it.

The example of the States called the "Latin Union"—that is, of France, Italy, Belgium, Switzerland, and Greece—is appealed to as a precedent for this policy, since they have limited their coinage of silver, as we have often explained. But their circumstances are very different from those of India. In France, which is so much the greatest, and also in Italy, inconvertible paper is really the ruling currency; it is that which settles prices, and everything has to conform to that. And even so the expedient is only regarded as a momentary one; it is acknowledged that the Latin Union must soon either return to the double standard, and coin silver without limit, or must demonetise silver altogether. And if we did not coin rupees, the fall in the price of silver which it would cause would probably determine them to decide on its demonetisation, whereas it is still possible that they may return to the double

* July 8, 1876.

standard, which would raise the price of silver more than anything else.

This possible effect on the Latin Union is, however, but a minor reason for not thinking of this, or any similar plan. The main reason is that the fall in silver will be greatly lessened if we allow the ordinary action of trade to spread it through the world, so that the depreciation may be everywhere alike, and affect prices everywhere where silver is the currency; and that all plans which impede that action tend to keep the silver in this market, to enhance its depreciation here, and to prevent its diffusion, which is the only cure.

VII.

THE REPORT OF THE COMMITTEE ON THE DEPRECIATION OF SILVER.

[From the "Economist" of July 15, 1876.]

The Report of the Commons Committee on the depreciation of silver is a very able document. It appears to have been drawn up by the chairman, Mr. Goschen, and accepted, with comparatively minor amendments, by the Committee,—and it has the clearness, the precision, and the great information—no matter at what labour acquired—for which Mr. Goschen's writings on such subjects are remarkable. The Committee was excluded, by the terms of its appointment, from investigating remedies *eo nomine*, but by describing precisely the events which have happened, and analysing, as far as is possible, the causes of each of those events, they have enormously facilitated the discussion of future policy. In all cases an accurate diagnosis of a disease must come before a discussion of remedies, and in a very complex case like this such a preliminary is especially needful, or else we may find that we have been trying to cure disease A with medicine fit only for disease B, and so have made things no better, or worse.

The most striking cause of the depreciation of silver, and that which the Committee treat of first, is the productiveness of the new mines in America. And looked at in this relation, the most remarkable thing about it is its rapidity. In former analogous cases the effect has been much slower. Adam Smith was of opinion that prices in England did not even *begin* to be sensibly affected by the American mines till 1570, though the first shipments of specie were made in 1502, and though the mines of Potosi—the most productive of all—were discovered in 1542. And even then the depreciation was slight, and continued to increase only at a slow rate for many years. When gold was discovered in our own time so extensively in California and in Australia, most persons thought it would at once affect general prices. But it did not. Even yet there is a controversy on the subject, and though we believe that, especially since Mr. Jevons' investigations, there can be little doubt that a rise in gold prices has happened to some extent, we should not like to state its extent precisely, and should fear to exaggerate it.

But now, the American mines were not much heard of in this country till last autumn, and the Committee tell us that the effect on the price of silver has been this :—

				d.		d.
1875	Yearly average		...	$56\frac{7}{8}$		
1876	Fluctuations in	January between	...	$56\frac{1}{8}$	and	$54\frac{7}{8}$
"	"	February "	...	$54\frac{7}{8}$	"	53
"	"	March "	...	$54\frac{1}{8}$	"	$52\frac{1}{2}$
"	"	April "	...	54	"	$53\frac{1}{2}$
"	"	May "	...	54	"	52
"	"	June "	...	52	"	50

and as we write it is 48d., showing a reduction of 16 per cent. from the average of 1875.

But we must observe that in this contrast we are

not comparing the same things. This table is a comparison of the price of silver with that of gold only; when we spoke of the previous discoveries we spoke of the general prices of comodities. But there is no evidence whatever that general prices in any country where prices are measured in silver have risen in any such ratio; indeed, as we have understood, careful inquiry seems to show that they have not sensibly risen at all. General prices have obeyed in this case the same law as in former cases; they are being acted on very slowly. Indeed, it is evident that they must be so; if they had risen 20 per cent. over the whole of the countries using silver as their principal currency, or over any very large part of them, 20 per cent. more on the silver currency used would have been wanted to circulate commodities at those prices, which, as there are few "economising expedients" in such countries, would have been a very large amount indeed. But no such new silver exists. The Committee say:—"It is, however, an important and remarkable fact, to which it may be convenient to call attention at once, that though the increased production of silver in the United States is a fact beyond question, no actual increase in the imports of silver from the United States to Great Britain has taken place since the year 1873, when the average price of silver was still 59¼d. per oz. Indeed, the amount of the imports into Great Britain from the United States for the year 1875, viz., £3,092,000, is the smallest since the year 1869. In the same way, though the new currency laws of Germany affected a vast silver coinage, the sales of silver actually made up to the 26th of April in the present year do not appear to have exceeded £6,000,000 distributed over several years."

Except a small amount of silver which goes from San Francisco to China direct, all the silver which leaves America comes here, and therefore it is plain that no such additional silver as would be required by very greatly raised prices over the large areas of the East anywhere exists. General prices there have not risen in any such ratio as 20 per cent.; what has alone so varied is the relation of silver to gold in the London market, and in the markets guided by it.

But even this variation is most curious. Nothing like it happened when gold was discovered in Australia and California. It did not fall then in relation to silver at all as silver has now fallen in relation to it. The course of prices then was this:—

	Per oz.—d.
In 1848 the average price of silver was	$59\frac{1}{2}$
1849 " "	$59\frac{3}{4}$
1850 " "	$60\frac{1}{16}$
1851 " "	61
1852 " "	$60\frac{1}{2}$
1853 " "	$61\frac{1}{2}$
1854 " "	$61\frac{1}{2}$
1855 " "	$61\frac{5}{16}$
1856 " "	$61\frac{5}{16}$

—which is certainly wonderfully little in comparison with what we now see, though the discoveries of gold then were every way as remarkable—indeed, more remarkable—than those of silver now. The difference is certainly not from any excessively quick supply now. As the Committee shows, in 1875 the silver sent from America was less than in previous years, and for the first six months of 1876 the figures have been these:—

IMPORT OF SILVER FROM UNITED STATES.

1874 (First six months)	... ...	£2,046,925
1875 ,,	... ...	1,293,258
1876 ,,	... ...	1,293,851

—so that, in fact, notwithstanding the great fall of silver in this market, owing in great part to the apprehension caused by the new mines, we have had from them no extra supply as yet at all.

The explanation is that the report of this new discovery came on a market where prices were previously falling, and which was most perturbed and sensitive. The Committee tell us that—

	d. d.
Between 1862 and 1866 the yearly average price was between	62 and 61
Between 1867 and 1872 the yearly average price was between	61 and 60
In 1873 the yearly average was	59¼
,, 1874 ,, ,, ...	$58\frac{5}{16}$
,, 1875 ,, ,, ...	56⅛

—showing a considerable fall. And they analyse the causes which were in action, weakening the temper of men's minds, and preparing them easily to allow of a still greater fall.

The first of these is the introduction of a gold currency into Germany in place of a silver one, of which the report gives a very clear and consecutive account. This cause, as our readers know, has been one peculiarly perturbing, because it has been incalculable as well as powerful. Dealers in silver have never for several years known either what quantity of it the German Government was anxious to dispose of, or what price it would take for that quantity. Nothing depresses the tone of a market like uncertainty, and this subterranean political agency, if we may so describe it, has now for a considerable period been a cause of uncertainty, in incessant action, and of the first magnitude. And its action still continues, for the amount of the thaler silver currency, which will have to be demonetised, is most uncertain, the estimates of it differing by many millions; and, therefore, we do not in the least know either what the German Government have in hand, or what they have to sell, or when they will have to sell it. The silver market is, consequently, affected exactly as the Liverpool cotton market would be if there was an immense unknown quantity to arrive. Such a market always, as the phrase is, lives from hand-to-mouth, sells as soon as it can, and the prices in it fall to an extent and with a rapidity which an observer, acquainted only with the visible supply or the visible demand, would not be able at all to account for.

The second cause is the policy of the Latin Union to which we have so often drawn the attention of our readers. The States comprising it—France, Belgium, Italy, Switzerland (and now Greece)—in 1873 adhered strictly to the principle of the double standard of gold and silver,—that is, they allowed any one to bring to the Mint any quantity of either metal, and they coined it for him. In consequence, at every change they were always coining the metal of lesser value, and that metal, when coined, was used to buy and take away the metal of higher value. In this way, during the cotton famine France was half emptied of silver which was wanted for export to the East, and was filled with gold which was not so wanted. If these States had continued to adhere to this principle, the great effect on the general silver market produced by the German operations would have been much diminished and rendered scarcely observable. As soon as silver began to fall it would have gone to France and been used there to buy gold which had risen. Thus silver would have been taken from the general market, and gold would have been brought to it, till the former level of comparative values, or something like it, had been reached. But France and the rest of the Latin Union could not endure this. Partly from political, and partly from economical motives, they would not take the "cast off" German silver. They limited the amount of the silver which they would coin, and thus the silver market was at the same moment perturbed by two extra-commercial causes: one set of countries sold off silver as they had never before done, and so increased the supply; and another refused to take it in a way in which they had never before done, and thus diminished the demand.

Thirdly, there has been another cause, also not commercial, though of a very different kind, which has tended to diminish the demand for silver. This is the increase in the amount which the Home Government draws for upon India, as to which the Committee tell us:—"The yearly amount payable by India for the disbursements of the Home Government has risen since the Indian Mutiny from £5,000,000 to £15,000,000, a difference of which the magnitude will be appreciated when it is remembered that it is considerably more than half of the total amount of silver annually produced.

"That the full effect of this substitution has only been recently felt, as that effect was retarded by the construction of the Indian railways, which involved an expenditure in India of money raised in England, counterbalancing therefore an equal amount of expenditure in England of money raised in India.

"That the amount of the disbursements which has just been stated appears to represent the present normal expenditure of the Home Government, and that, therefore, unless by some marked change of policy, no diminution of that amount can be looked for."

The effect of this increase of the *tribute*, for such economically it is, which India pays to England is peculiar, because the ordinary relation of the two countries commercially has been peculiar. Generally the existence of such a tribute makes no difference in the amount of the precious metals transmitted from one country to the other. Mr. Mill explains this very clearly. "Commerce," he says, "being supposed to be in a state of equilibrium when the obligatory remittances begin, the first remittance is necessarily made in money. This lowers prices in the remitting country, and raises them in the receiving. The natural effect is that more commodities are exported than before, and fewer imported; and that, on the score of commerce alone, a balance of money will be constantly due from the receiving to the paying country. When the debt thus annually due to the tributary country becomes equal to the annual tribute or other regular payment due from it, no further transmission of money takes place; the equilibrium of exports and imports will no longer exist, but that of payments will; the exchange will be at par, the two debts will be set off against one another, and the tribute or remittance will be virtually paid in goods."

But in the case of this increase of the tribute from India to England, the primary supposition of Mr. Mill does not hold. The exchanges were not before in what he calls "equilibrium"—that is, one which did not admit of a transmission either way of the precious metals. There was a constant export of silver from England to India—a sum of money constantly paid by the dominant to the dependent country. And in such case the effect of an increase of the sum due from the dependency almost always at first is, and perhaps may permanently continue to be, a diminution of the cash which the superior country has to transmit. This is one effectual mode of rectifying the balance; it is the simplest, it is always the first taken. And it has been so here. From a most careful and valuable examination in the Committee's report, it appears that—

Between 1868-9 and 1871-2, the annual average export of silver to India from England was	£10,000,000
Ditto ditto 1872-3 and 1875-6 ...	4,100,000
Diminution	£5,900,000

But on the other hand, the increase in the "tribute money," as we call it, or the Government drafts, is:—

Between 1872-3 and 1875-6, the average of Government bills on India was... ...	£12,600,000
Ditto ditto 1868-9 and 1871-2	7,400,000
Increase	£5,200,000

And the diminution in the demand for silver thus caused has been weighing on the silver market, making it constantly sensitive, and tending more and more to reduce the price.

These, with some minor ones on which we cannot dwell, are the causes why the silver discoveries now have produced so much more sudden an effect on the bullion market, that is, on the relative value of silver to gold, than the gold discoveries did on the relation of gold to silver five-and-twenty years ago. And surprising as that difference is, they are fully sufficient to account for it.

As to the discoveries themselves, the Committee speak with much caution. They very properly abstained from calling evidence from persons connected with the mines, as otherwise their report might have been made a "puffing machine," to raise the price of the shares in particular companies. They rely on the official documents which the American Government issued, the contents of which we have, we believe, laid before our readers from time to time.

They estimate the total yield of the United States:—

Average annual yield from 1864 to 1867 ...	£2,300,000
Yield in 1872	5,750,000
„ 1874	6,400,000
„ 1875 (perhaps)	6,400,000
„ 1876 „	9,000,000

These figures are not very large, and would come to very little when distributed over all the countries of the world which use silver as their standard of value, and in comparison with gold the effect is less, because the yield of gold from the new mines is itself very large. "Mr. Whitehill, the State Mineralogist" for the State of Nevada, the Committee tells us, "states that, 'during the past two years (1873 and 1874) this mine has yielded bullion to the value of 5,000,000 dollars, the principal of it since last June. The yield for September was 562,000 dollars, and for October 610,000 dollars. The daily yield of the ore is about 400 tons; about 44 per cent. of the value of the bullion is gold.'"

If in the end the supply of gold from these mines is increased on a sudden nearly equally with that of silver, the ultimate effects will not be at all like that which the recent state of prices has shown.

Now, from full information, we see the nature of the evil from which we are suffering. We are not suffering from a depreciation of silver as against commodities in the countries where silver is the standard value, for there is no supply sufficient to produce such a depreciation, nor time if there had been such a supply to diffuse it, and there is no such depreciation in fact. We are not suffering from a depreciation of silver as against gold caused by a sudden excess in the supply of silver, for the new supplies of silver have been only moderate, and none of them have come here. We are not suffering from a depreciation of silver as against gold caused by a diminution in the cost of production of silver, for there has been no time, or anything approaching to time, to say what the ultimate cost of production will be. No doubt certain mines of singular fertility have been discovered, but it is not silver produced in the best mine which determines the price of silver, as a whole, any more than it is the corn grown on the best land which determines the price of corn as a whole;

that which does determine it is the cost of production in the worst mine which can maintain itself in working. The producer in the least favourable circumstances always fixes the price; those in better circumstances take that price, and get an extra profit. And what that mine will be in the case of silver we cannot as yet tell; the experience of years alone can determine it. All that we can now safely say is that, judging from all past similar events, it will not be any of the new mines now discovered, or any of fertility approaching to theirs, but some other far down in the scale, some one which has been in some degree better than some others till now, and therefore will be able to maintain itself when those others are obliged to desist from working.

What we are suffering from is the apprehension of increased production of silver suddenly supervening on a market previously perturbed, upon which one Government had forced an extra supply, from which a union of other Governments had refused to take, as usual, any supply, and in which another Government, by an increase of the tribute it requires from a silver-importing country, has temporarily, if not permanently, lessened the demand.

This explanation of the real malady at once disposes of a crowd of unreal remedies. No competent person can propose a demonetisation of silver in India, and a substitution of gold for it, just at a moment when the price of silver has been thrust down by so strong an apprehension caused by such peculiar circumstances. It would be to require the Indian Government to buy the largest amount of gold ever bought in the dearest market for gold, and to dispose of the largest amount of silver in the cheapest market for silver, which ever existed. The present financial position of the Indian Government is no doubt impaired by this sudden depreciation of the metal in which it receives its revenue; but the remedy for a minor deficit would bring in, in lieu of it, a deficit of the first magnitude; it would be nothing else but financial ruin.

Again, no one would propose to arrest coining silver in the East as a remedy for such a state of things, for this would only disorder the silver market still further. It would add a new political difficulty to those previous political difficulties which have caused so much disturbance, and so make the existing confusion far worse than before. Nor can it be maintained that the Indian Government should now require the ryot, whose rent has been formerly fixed in silver, to pay either in gold itself, or in so much more silver as would purchase the same quantity of gold as that fixed rent would have purchased when the settlement was made. If silver in India had become depreciated as against commodities in general, it might have been possible to say to the ryot, "You are selling your commodities for more silver, and therefore it is not unfair to ask you to pay us—the Government—a proportionate amount more." Even then the ryot would have been probably discontented; he would have said, "If prices had gone down, the Government would never have let me off, and it is not fair that they should take the benefit of good times when they leave me the misfortune of hard times." Still, in this case, if the depreciation of silver had been against commodities in general, it would have been perhaps substantially, though not intelligibly, equitable to adopt such a policy. But now that there is no such depreciation of silver as compared with commodities, such a scheme is not feasible. The ryot in India does not sell his produce a bit dearer than he did a year ago; his income, as yet, is just what it was, and it must be so till a vast amount of silver has gone to India to raise the prices of daily life. Clearly, therefore, he must not be additionally taxed because the silver market is apprehensive, and because certain Governments (the Indian Government being one of them) have perturbed it.

The real remedy, as we have shown several times, is to leave the great natural forces of trade to operate unrestricted. The true remedy for an enfeebled market is an access of demand, and in this case the laws of commerce, if not suspended or crippled by State interference, will produce that demand. The necessary effect of a depreciation of silver as against gold is to give a bounty on exports from India and the other silver-using countries to England. An English merchant can now buy many more rupees than he formerly could with the same number of sovereigns, and therefore he can import from India, though prices at Calcutta are not at a level at which it would have paid him to operate if he had not had that novel facility in getting rupees. Similarly, shippers to India cannot afford to sell at the same price in rupees which they could have formerly, for they will lose in bringing those rupees home. And the combined effect of this bounty on exports from India, and of this fine on imports into India, must sooner or later be an unfavourable balance of trade, and a consequent flow of silver to the East. A new demand of great magnitude will eventually relieve the silver market, if we only leave it alone.

It has been objected that as yet this process has not begun. But in this complexly organised world, it is never safe to reason that a force, even of great magnitude, does not exist because its effect may be impeded. No doubt, as the first table we print at the end of this article shows, the exports from India to this country have in many instances not increased, though in some they have; but then table No. 2 shows why. The prices of those articles in England have gone down, and, therefore, though there might be a gain in comparison with last year on the exchange, there might be a loss as compared with last year on the whole transaction. As to the diminution of profitableness of shipments *to* India from hence, there is, unhappily, no doubt. Every trade circular dealing with the East records — every Chamber of Commerce in cities interested in the East resounds with complaints—that it is so. Sooner or later this must cause a large diminution in that branch—a diminution, no doubt, universally to be much regretted, but nevertheless an evil necessary to be endured, because it is part of the appropriate remedy at the present time. We have spoken of India because that is the silver-using country which comes most easily to an Englishman's mouth; but the same thing is true of China, of the whole East, and of every other part of the world. To them all, there must ere long be an export of silver. In a time when the speculative part of the business world were eager and animated, this would have happened long ere this; but even the present indisposition to begin new things, and the recent ruin of so many of those who were most disposed to do so, cannot long delay it.

At what price silver will settle down, nothing but experience can determine; but the two cardinal points in the matter are—first, that that price will be determined by the cost in the *least* good mine which pays to keep at work; secondly, that the extra demand for silver to countries where it is the standard money will require a very large sum, if the value of silver as against commodities is to be depreciated in all of them, because the efficiency of a metal as money depends on it. By whatever per-centage you depreciate it, you make it necessary by that very per-centage, *cæteris paribus*, to have more of it. And as the quantity of silver now circulating is immense, even a small per-centage on it comes to a good sum, so that ultimately mines of far inferior grade to those now so much talked of will continue to be worked, will settle the value of silver, regulate its price, and in all likelihood prevent any such depreciation of it as the peculiar perturbations of the present moment have led many to apprehend.

TABLE OF PRINCIPAL ARTICLES IMPORTED INTO THE UNITED KINGDOM FROM BRITISH INDIA.

	First Half-Year			
	1876.	1875.	Increase.	Decrease.
Wheat ... ...cwts.	1,166,000 ...	119,000 ...	1,047,000 ...	...
Cotton ... ... ,,	1,152,000 ...	1,617,000 ...	...	... 465,000
Hemp ... ... ,,	29,000 ...	57,000 ...	...	... 28,000
Hides, dry ... ... ,,	187,000 ...	218,000 ...	...	... 31,000
Seed, flax, and linseed ,,	603,000 ...	205,000 ...	398,000 ...	...
Silk, raw ... ... lbs.	89,000 ...	244,000 ...	...	... 155,000
Sugar, unrefined ...cwts.	47,000 ...	205,000 ...	...	... 158,000
Tea ... ... lbs.	9,903,000 ...	10,708,000 ...	...	... 805,000
Wool, sheep, and lambs ,,	13,117,000 ...	10,194,000 ...	2,923,000 ...	...

AVERAGE PRICES OF IMPORTS FROM BRITISH INDIA.

		First Half-Year 1876.			First Half-Year 1875.			Increase.		Decrease.	
		£	s.	d.	£	s.	d.	s.	d.	s.	d.
Wheat	per cwt.	0	10	0	0	9	5	0	7	...	
Cotton	"	2	9	6	2	15	0	...		5	6
Hemp	"	0	19	5	1	1	9	...		2	4
Hides, dry	"	3	15	0	3	19	9	...		4	9
Seed, flax and linseed	per qr.	2	9	3	2	14	3	...		5	0
Tea	per lb.	0	1	8⅜	0	1	9⅛	...		0	0¾
Wool	"	0	0	9¾	0	0	10¼	...		0	0½

VIII.

THE PROPOSAL OF THE BENGAL CHAMBER OF COMMERCE TO SUSPEND THE COINAGE OF SILVER IN INDIA.

[From the "Economist" of August 5, 1876.]

The Chamber of Commerce of Bengal have resolved "that it is expedient for the Government to suspend clause 19 of Act 23 of 1870, which makes it obligatory on the Indian Mint to receive all silver tendered for coinage;" as also "section 1 of clause 11 of Act 3 of 1871, which makes it obligatory on the Currency Department to issue notes against silver bullion sent in, and that during such suspension it be unlawful to import coined rupees." The weight of the authority of that Chamber has, therefore, been given to the proposal to suspend the coinage of silver, and thus to maintain the value of the rupee by diminishing the numbers of it in circulation, although the silver out of which it is made is falling in value.

The effect of this plan would be, as is obvious, to hold out the greatest stimulus to private coinage which has ever been given in the world. The basis of the whole proceeding is that the silver as a metal is likely to fall much and rapidly in value, in consequence of the new mines in America. But if this is so, the Americans will not lose the Indian market if they can help it. If the Government will not coin these rupees they will do it for themselves, and no law will be able to keep what they coin out of India.

We have also proved that this plan would have the necessary effect of suspending the natural cure for the present evil. The silver market is now disorganised, not by a great supply, but by an excessive apprehension. And the proper cure for such a market (and it is often a rapid one) is a brisk demand. Now the nature of the present fall in the exchange value of the rupee is, as has been at length explained, to give a bounty on exports from India, to give a discouragement to imports into India, and thus to create a balance of trade favourable to India, and a flow of silver thither. As there is no excess of supply in the silver market, the demand thus created will greatly sustain its value.

But there are other objections than these to the plan which, as they arise from its bad effect on Indian trade, should have prevented the Bengal Chamber of Commerce from recommending it. A metallic currency, of which the quantity is artificially regulated, of which whoever likes cannot get as much coined as he wishes, is as much a currency of fictitious value as a currency of inconvertible paper —and a nation which takes it is exposed to the same evil. A rupee "limited"—that is to say, a rupee of which the numbers could not by law be augmented —would do in India much what the greenback has done in America. It would be an appreciated artificial currency, instead of a depreciated artificial one, but it would be an obstacle to commerce, and would tend to isolate the country exactly in the same way.

In dealing with America now, as we need not explain, there are two problems for the English exporter; he has to consider for how many greenbacks he can sell his article, and then how much "sterling exchange" he can buy with those greenbacks. In dealing with a country which has a metallic currency there is always a limit to the fluctuations of exchange. The premium on bills can never rise beyond "the specie point"—the point at which it will pay to export gold or silver, as the case may be. But in the case of a fictitious currency, there is no such final point, for that currency cannot be exported. The premium on bills may rise to any height, as the depreciated paper is more and more multiplied. Upon an average, any extra high paper-price for his article obtained in America by the English merchant will be compensated by an equal loss on turning the paper into sterling. When other things rise in paper-price, the paper-price of gold as a rule will rise too, and with it the price of bills on London payable in gold. But though this is the general tendency, and a perfectly sure tendency on the average, it is only so sure on the average; it may fail in a particular case, and very often does. During the Civil War, and at other times when gold has been an article of great speculation, the fluctuations in the premium on it have been very violent. And there were no corresponding fluctuations in commodities because there was no similar speculation in them. At other times there might be speculation in commodities not shared by gold or bills. And thus the whole trade is confused. The profit is uncertain, because it depends in the long run on the counterbalancing effect of two bargains, and very often the two do not counterbalance.

All persons engaged in the American trade are most anxious to get rid of this impediment, but the effect of the scheme of the Bengal Chamber would be to introduce into the Indian trade a similar impediment—only, so to speak, with the other side turned up. Prices in India would fall, not rise, in consequence of the non-coinage of the rupee. We must remember that the currency of a stationary country requires constant renewal, and that of a progressive country requires constant increase; and therefore, if you keep the quantity fixed, prices are sure to fall. And as the rupee cannot be imported, there is no check on this fall. Smuggling rupees apart—the decline will continue so long as the fixity in quantity of the rupee is maintained, and it will be quicker or slower in proportion as the increase of the country is so.

No doubt the price of bills on England will in the long run fall too, like that of other things. There will be less money as a rule coming to England, because English imports into India have sold for less. But there will be no reliance on this being so in any particular case. The trade will be in confusion. As long as silver can pass as money between the two countries, there is a limit to fluctuation in exchange; but the moment you limit the coinage of the rupee, you prevent that passage. Silver, if the Bengal Chamber have their way, will be quoted with incessant fluctuations in Calcutta, just as gold is in New York, and its price and that of bills payable in it will be as much liable to the influence of speculation.

Though, on the whole, this appreciation of the coin-rupee would probably be better than the depreciation of the greenback, its first effects would be more painful. The fall in prices would make people think that they were getting poorer; whereas, in the opposite case, the rise makes them imagine they are getting richer. And the "contraction," as Americans call it, would raise the rate of interest. There would be less money to lend, just as in the case of depreciation there is more money to lend—again a painful effect instead of a pleasant. Both are temporary; the change of prices makes the desire of persons to borrow less in the one case or more in the other, and that change likewise makes their power of borrowing less or greater, because the value of securities decreases or increases. Still, for the time, the first effect of an appreciation is not pleasant, and neither the Indian nor any other mercantile community which has been exposed to it has ever liked it.

And then, what is to be the end? Either the depreciation of silver depends on passing causes, and then this appreciation is needless—it would be better not to disturb the ordinary course of trade; or, on the other hand, the depreciation of silver is more or less to be permanent, and then this appreciation of the rupee is mischievous. It will cause a motion of prices in the wrong direction to the natural one. It will cause prices to fall just when, from the legitimate effect of circumstances, they should rise. And this wrong movement will have to be corrected; this artificial rise will have to be undone; and so, in addition to the inevitable fall of the value of the rupee *with* that of silver, there will be a needless fall of the rupee *to* that of silver.

An idea seems indistinctly to float in many minds that in this way an opportunity will be obtained for introducing gold. But how will it be gained? The difficulty of introducing gold in place of silver is that you must demonetise silver, and give gold in place of it. But the silver is so great in amount that the Indian Government could hardly get gold to replace it, and could never afford the cost of the change. No doubt there would be fewer rupees in circulation the longer the coinage was suspended; but then each of these rupees would be of higher value as coin than as silver, and when it came after the demonetisation to be sold as silver there would be so much extra loss.

It is asked, too, why should not we do in India as the Latin Union do in Europe; why should we not assume their "expectant attitude?" But the cases are not similar. In India, silver is practically the only legal tender; in France and Italy, it is one of three, and in the rest of the Latin Union, one of two. The main currency in the first two countries, which are by far the greater and richer part of the Latin Union, is inconvertible paper, which is now really the standard, and not metal at all. And in the other countries gold circulates as well as silver, so that practically, silver is only a subordinate currency in the Latin Union, taking it as a whole, and therefore the limitation of its quantity does not cause prices to fall, for prices are not measured in it. The scale is so much smaller too, that false coining has not yet operated, any more than it does in our own token coinage. And the whole position is different. The Latin Union was a group of double-standard countries largely using gold, and the question for them is whether they will give up their gold and become silver countries exclusively — which would happen if they were to abandon the limitation of coinage while silver is as cheap as now—or whether they will demonetise silver and use gold as a standard only. This would be troublesome and costly, but still it could be done. But India has no problem to consider; she is irrevocably committed to a sole silver currency, and therefore a similar attitude would in her case, besides being mischievous, have no meaning.

The true remedy, as we have often shown, is not to impede silver's going to India, but to permit the laws of trade to diffuse silver through India and through the world. This will cause an immense demand for silver, for the countries where it is the only currency are still vast and numerous.

IX.

THE DEBATE ON THE INDIAN BUDGET.

[From the "Economist" of August 12, 1876.]

The whole interest of the debate on the Indian Budget centred in the discussion on the value of silver. Independently of this, the finances of India were in a fairly good position—as compared with that of most Governments in the world, a very good one. It is true that if you include the amount expended on reproductive works, there is a deficit of about two millions last year, and that there always is a large one. But then few other Governments make any similar expenditure, and treat it in the Budget as the Indian Government does, and for many purposes this way of spending money must be separated from others. It is at least *meant* to be an investment, which no other kind of Government expenditure is, and you have to discuss in relation to it commercial questions of profit and loss, with which in the accounts of Governments you have ordinarily nothing to do. With these we need not now meddle; those who at this moment care most for the matter, care for it in relation to the depreciation of silver, and to nothing else.

Lord George Hamilton estimated the loss by exchange at £2,312,000 for the year 1876-7, but he did not expect a deficit as against the *ordinary* expenditure in consequence. On the contrary, he reckoned—

Revenue	£50,480,000
Ordinary expenditure	50,336,000
Surplus	£144,000

—a result which he said was very good, and which, no doubt, is so, if (which we do not now deny) the extraordinary expenditure is good and proper.

This loss on exchange arises, as the report of Mr. Goschen's Committee showed, in two ways; first, from the depreciation of silver; and next, from the increase of the Council drafts—of what may be called the tribute from India. As to the first, Lord George explained very clearly that the Government had no intention of touching now any of the remedies which have been proposed—either the suspension of silver coinage, or the introduction of a gold one, or an adjustment of the land revenue. And he assigned what seem to us to be excellent reasons for so doing, which we need not, however, give at length, as we have at various times placed them before our readers. He said, too, what is well known, but what it is nevertheless desirable to have confirmed by official authority, that the natural remedies were operating, that the price of Indian commodities measured in silver had not risen, and that in consequence a great encouragement had been given to the exports from India, which would cause a demand for silver here, and would relieve the market. And we may now expect that this process will go on more rapidly than before. One great cause of hesitation has been the fear that Government might "do something," something that might be anything, and which would derange the usual course of business. But now that the wise policy of the Government has been announced, there will no longer be any such fear of disturbance.

Mr. Goschen added on this point the weight of his authority—especially great, as having recently elaborately investigated the whole subject, as chairman of the late committee—to that of the Government. He showed at length that none of the plans which had been proposed were at present at all fit for adoption. And he said especially that he had seen statistics which seemed to show that prices had not risen in India, which all other information confirms. And even without statistics, common-sense would show that such is likely to have been the case. A great rise in the price of all commodities through a country using a metallic currency only requires a great increase in that currency to carry itno. But no such amounts of silver have gone to India, or anything like them, as the following figures show :—

IMPORTS OF SILVER INTO INDIA.

Net Imports (after deducting Exports).

In 1866-67	£6,960,000
1867-68	5,590,000
1868-69	8,600,900
1869-70	7,320,000
1870-71	940,000
1871-72	6,515,000
1872-73	705,000
1873-74	2,450,000
1874-75	4,640,000
And in the year just concluded, *i.e.*, 1875-76	1,555,000

And therefore silver prices cannot have risen, for

there has been no silver to raise them with. The indisposition to admit this arises from not understanding the distinction between the depreciation of silver, which we elsewhere explain,* as against gold in a market where it is not a money, and its depreciation as against commodities in a market where it *is* a money. When this distinction is clearly seen there is no longer any difficulty in this part of the subject.

As to the second element in the loss by exchange —the "tribute," as it may be called—the Government stand in a very different position. They are bound to do something here, for they have to bring home their money from India. But they are not bound to bring it home except in the way in which they lose the least—or rather, they *are* bound to bring it home in that way. There could be no objection at times to their lending money in India and borrowing it at home at the same moment, if the time did not appear favourable for bringing it home. And they can choose any mode of remittance they think best; it is merely a matter of business, like the remittance of any other money. And this Lord George Hamilton very well explained. Of course, however, the finance policy of the Government should be calculable, and the amounts for which it is going to draw on India should be made known some time in advance, as otherwise they will make business uncertain, and so diminish it.

* See Chapter X.

X.

THE DIFFERENT EFFECT ON TRADE OF A CHEAPENING OF THE PRECIOUS METALS, AND OF A DEPRECIATION OF INCONVERTIBLE PAPER.

[FROM THE "ECONOMIST" OF AUGUST 12, 1876.]

WE showed last week that neither the depreciation of an inconvertible paper, nor the appreciation of an artifically limited coin, produces as a rule any effect on trade. What an English exporter to America gains on the one hand, in the additional price for his goods, consequent on the depreciation of greenbacks, he loses on the other, by the additional price which he has to pay for gold, or a bill payable in gold, which he requires to bring that price to England. Greenbacks are of no use here, and their depreciation upon an average, though by no means always in every particular case, affects the prices equally of all things. It is a local depreciation, beginning in a particular country, affecting alike all the property and products of that country, but affecting nothing out of it.

But it is necessary to distinguish this most carefully from a depreciation of the precious metals caused by a large new supply. That new supply is a new exportable product, sent from the country of its origin through the world, and thus affects more or less, in proportion to its magnitude, the world's trade.

Suppose, for simplicity, that silver were the *only* precious metal in the world—that all nations used it as money, and that none of them used gold in that way at all—the process of depreciation by such new supplies as are expected from Nevada would be this: prices in Nevada and in the rest of the United States would rise; in consequence, imports into the United States would tend to increase, exports from them would tend to decrease, and so an unfavourable "balance of trade," as the phrase is, being created, silver would be exported; it would be the best way in which America could pay for her imports, and she would so pay for them. On the other hand, the country from which those imports came—suppose it was India—would receive that silver, and in proportion as it received more and more, its prices would be more and more raised. What happened, in consequence of the new silver, in the country of its origin, will again happen in the country of its first receipt. Imports into that country will be stimulated, exports from it checked, an unfavourable balance of trade created, and silver will be sent to the countries which it has to pay. Then, in their turn, these countries—the countries of second receipt, as we may call them—will undergo all the same changes. The depreciation of a depreciated paper is a stationary depreciation, fixed in the country which makes the paper; but that of a precious metal is a *travelling* depreciation, which passes slowly over the civilised world, altering trade everywhere, creating a new article of export, first from one country and then another, and in consequence, generating a new trade of export to pay for it in the country which receives it.

The *modus operandi* of this process is much affected in the usual state of the world by there being two precious metals used as money—gold and silver—and also by gold being in many ways the principal of the two; but though the detail is changed, the principle is the same. In a country which uses gold only as a standard currency, silver is a commodity having its price only in gold, just as silk or cotton; that price goes up and down in the same way, and is quoted in the same way. And London is the principal centre of the wholesale commerce, and especially of the new wholesale commerce, of the world. We buy more readily than any other nation, for we have much more money than any other of equal enterprise; and, therefore, all great business requiring new capital on a sudden comes here. Accordingly, the new silver for the most part goes not straight to India and the East, where it is a money, but to England, where it is a common article, and we send it over the world and to the nations where it is a money. But this is only a change in the *route* of the depreciation. It interposes a sort of house of call, it does not change the essence of the matter.

No doubt the first effect has been to advertise and make far more obvious than it would otherwise have been the depreciation of silver. If silver had been our money, as gold is, we should scarcely have been as yet conscious of its being depreciated. A few millions more silver (from Germany or elsewhere) would have gone into the Bank, would have eased the Money Market, and have tended to raise prices. And we should have had to pay for that silver, just as we pay for the gold which *does* come. But this process would have been very gradual—probably, as yet, nearly unfelt. The ready demand for silver as a currency in England would have much maintained its value here. You could not have depreciated it much without increasing its quantity—both the quantity in the Bank and the quantity in out-of-door circulation—very largely. But as silver is not a money (except as a token), not a money regulating prices, not a money which more and more is wanted as the value falls more and more, there has been no new English demand of equal or comparable size. Some more silver may, in consequence of the cheapness, have been taken for the arts, but this is all. The actual supply from Germany and the apprehended supply from America have come to a market which other circumstances had made bare of demand. They generated no new demand, and in consequence, there is a great fall in the value of silver in England. The travelling depreciation has come here, and has been intensified, as has been shown.

This sudden fall in the value of silver in England has caused a corresponding alteration in the exchange with the countries whose money is silver. As is well known, between two countries which use the same metal for money, there is a natural and fixed par of exchange. A certain weight of that metal of a certain fineness, in the currency of one of these countries, will always exchange for an equal weight of like quality in the currency of the other. But between two countries, one which employs gold and the other silver, there is no such natural par. The relation between the two currencies depends on the amount of the one metal which will exchange for a given amount of the other. When, as now, that amount much varies in England, there is an immediate change in the relation of the English gold currency to foreign silver currencies, because the amount of gold which it would take here to buy any given amount of silver, to export it and coin it into those silver currencies, varies.

And this is the process by which the depreciation travels on another step. Silver being cheaper here, more of it will be bought and sent to the countries where silver is money. But its value there against commodities will not fall as suddenly as it has here. We see that it would not, if silver had been the only metal used as money in the world. And the countries where it is used are, within their own boundaries, in the same position. The more silver falls in purchasing power, the more of it will be wanted to purchase commodities, and the demand for it, therefore, will increase incessantly where the supply is augmented. The silver prices of commodities will be slowly raised everywhere where silver is money, and a great deal of it will be required in the process, and the course of trade will be changed. The silver countries must find exports to pay for this new article, silver, which is coming in upon them.

We must, therefore, carefully distinguish two things which are often confounded in discussing this subject. First, we must see that a depreciation of a metal used as money, whether silver or gold, is utterly different in its effects from those of a depreciation of a currency of paper, for it creates an international trade, and that of paper a local one only.

Secondly, we must see that the depreciation of silver in London, where it is only a commodity, is a wholly different thing from its depreciation in countries where it is a money. The first, as we have seen, is very rapid, but the second is very slow indeed. And the second will counteract the effect of the first, as it is now daily doing, and will tend to raise the value of silver in London—in the *entrepôt*—where the market is so sensitive, by distributing it over vast regions where much more will be wanted if the value falls comparatively but a little.

Thirdly, we must observe that this process is not at all bad for the trade of England. No doubt the fall in the rate of exchange is a disadvantage to shippers to the countries where money is silver. But then another class of exporters will be benefited, for we import that silver, and have to pay for it. The loss, on the other hand, will be counterbalanced by a gain on the other.

XI.

THE AMERICAN COMMISSION ON THE CURRENCY.

[From the "Economist," of September 21, 1876.]

The last act of the Congress was to appoint a Commission, to consider and report on the currency question in its various present bearings, that is,—

"First, into the change which has taken place in the relative value of gold and silver; the causes thereof; whether permanent or otherwise; the effects thereof upon trade, commerce, finance, and productive interests of the country, and upon the standard of value in this and foreign countries:

"Second, into the policy of the restoration of the double standard in this country, and if restored, what the legal relation between the two coins, silver and gold, should be:

"Third, into the policy of continuing legal-tender notes concurrently with the metallic standards, and the effects thereof upon the labour, industries, and wealth of the country; and,

"Fourth, into the best means of providing for facilitating the resumption of specie payments."

And this Commission will, no doubt, be of use to European economists in collecting information as to many American matters connected with the currency, upon which it is now very difficult to find a trustworthy authority. But as far as respects the practical questions to be determined in the United States, "half would have been more than the whole;" it would—at least, if we may judge as this distance—have been much better to have restricted the Commission to fewer points, than to empower them, as has been practically done, to inquire into anything and everything as to American currency. In the heat of a Presidential contest, the Commission must be active-minded indeed if they can thoroughly work out all this.

The set of facts most wanting inquiry certainly is the new set—that relating to the change in the value of silver. The conditions of resumption—the mode in which a satisfactory paper currency should be maintained after resumption—are old matters, on which American statesmen can find no difficulty in obtaining information quite as good as this Commission will collect for them. But the present relative position of silver and gold is a perfectly new thing in the world, and America, as a principal producer of both, and as having to settle whether she will have a currency of both or either, ought certainly to investigate it as soon and as completely as possible.

The cardinal present novelty is that silver and gold are, in relation to one another, simply ordinary commodities. Until now they have not been so. A very great part of the world adhered to the bi-metallic system, which made both gold and silver legal tenders, and which established a fixed relation between them. In consequence, whenever the value of the two metals altered, these countries acted as equalising machines. They took the metal which fell; they sold the metal which rose; and thus the relative value of the two was kept at its old point. But now this curious mechanism is broken up. There is no great country now really acting on this system. The "Latin Union," it is true, adhere to the name, but they have abandoned the thing. As they do not allow silver to be coined except in limited quantities, they have no longer an equalising action; they no longer receive the depreciated or part with the appreciated metal, and, therefore, the two metals now exchange for one another, just as other commodities. The gold-price of silver is now like the gold-price of tin—left practically, for the first time in history, without artificial regulation, and free from the manipulation of Governments. And it is into the consequences of this that the United States should now inquire, for they have nowhere been fully treated of.

The first effect is that to which M. Léon Say drew attention not long ago, in a speech of much ability—the *instability* of the value of the two metals. In former times, he justly said that the fluctuations in the relative value of the two metals were few and small, but now they are many and large. Particular causes, no doubt, aggravate that instability at this moment—especially the demonetisation of silver by Germany, and the supposed likelihood of great supplies from Nevada. But though the instability is aggravated by these causes, it is not created by them, and it will not cease with them. There is no inherent reason why the gold price of silver should be uniform, any more than why the gold price of platinum should be the same. The old notion of extreme steadiness is one generated by the practice of Governments, and which has ceased when the practice ceased, and will not revive till it revives.

The United States, therefore, which have a "money" to choose, must observe that they have three courses to choose from, and must see what are the consequences of each. First—they may choose the old bi-metallic, or double-standard plan. But if they do, they must make up their mind to be always changing their coinage. The natural value of the two metals now being, as we see, fluctuating, a nation which takes both will be incessantly changing from one to the other—it will always be taking the worse and giving the better. The existence of such a country, or set of countries, is an advantage to the world at large, because, as we have seen, it preserves a uniformity between the two metals, one or other of which is used by all civilised nations to count value. But the expense and inconvenience of a changing currency are great, and how far a nation would be wise to undergo them for the good of the world, we are not sure. She herself obtains no advantage; she sells gold for silver, or silver for gold, and the brokers get their commission; but this is all. And to a great borrowing nation like America, it would always be an objection that she would pay in the worse coin at the time of payment, whatever it might be. At the present moment, America would become a silver country, and the interest and principal on her obligations would be paid in silver. The evil, of course, would not be what the momentary circumstances of the market would now suggest. Silver would not be at 52d. per ounce if America was a country with a sole silver currency. So large a demand as her coin requirements would send the price up very rapidly—perhaps to its old amount. Still, as the debts of America are so large, the probable objection which a lender might make to the certainty of his having to accept the inferior mode of repayment is to her important; she would possibly have to borrow on terms somewhat less good.

Secondly—the United States might take the single gold standard like ourselves; and this is what, till very lately, every English economist would have advised them to do. The evils of this plan had not then been seen, but its good was very apparent. That all great commercial nations should have the same metal for money is, *per se*, a plain gain. The objection is that there may be some difficulty in getting the gold for so many, very rapidly. The total production of gold, according to the estimate laid before the Silver Committee, for recent years is:—

In 1872	£17,569,000
1873	21,946,000
1874	19,880,000
1875	20,353,000
Total	£79,748,000

or nearly £20,000,000 a year. And this is not at all a large amount to provide for the yearly uses of the world.

In the 13 years from 1858-75 the imports of gold into the United Kingdom were	£331,179,000
Exports from	251,413,000
Total absorption in 18 years	£79,766,000

or at the rate of £4,432,000 a year, being more than

one-fifth of the whole. So that if Germany, America, and perhaps the Latin Union, were all to take to a gold currency, there would certainly not be too much gold. Probably the money markets of the world would be straitened by there not being sufficient.

The third and last course open to the United States is to make silver their sole standard. A few weeks ago this would have been generally deemed to be beyond the limits of consideration; at that time there was a panic, and it was imagined that the price of silver was going to fall lower and lower till it became worth hardly anything. But experience has now shown, as theory always suggested, that there would be a demand for silver for the East consequent on its cheapness—that this demand would grow with its cheapness—and then an almost indefinite quantity, if supplied, would in time be taken off the market. As the supply here is small, the price has risen rapidly, though it has for a moment been checked again by the financial operations of the Council of India in drawing for their tribute. The extreme panic as to the price of silver has, therefore, passed away, and we are able to consider calmly whether it would be wise for the United States to take it for a standard of value or not.

If they did, it is certain that the price of silver would for the moment rise, because so very large an extra quantity would at once be required; and it is very possible that this price might not again fall. The final regulator of the price of silver is the cost at which it can be produced in the least fertile mine that can maintain itself in working. At the present moment, there are new mines as to whose extent there are very various accounts, which may supersede some of the worst of those at work, and so lessen the maximum cost of the production of silver—the cost which fixes its price. But if so large a new demand for silver as that for supplying the United States with money were added to the existing demands, very possibly the extra fertility of these new mines might be exhausted before that demand was satisfied. These mines might come to be not so much better than the old mines as to throw any old mine out of work; and if so, the price of silver would remain what it formerly was. And if this happened, silver would be as good a standard of value as it has ever been.

There would, undoubtedly, be several difficulties in the adoption of a silver standard by the United States. First—Much of the interest of their Debt is now payable in gold coin. This would not, however, cause much difficulty, if the price of silver were to rise, as we have suggested, to something like the old level. The United States might then either continue to receive their Customs' duties, as they now do, in gold only, and to pay their interest with such gold, or they might pay an equivalent in silver. The difficulty would be one of detail only, and might be met.

Secondly—what is more serious—the trade between the United States and the gold-using countries would be liable to be disturbed by every fluctuation in the value of gold and silver. And we are not yet in a position to say what the amount of this inconvenience would be, because the changes in the relative values of the two will in future probably be greater and more frequent than they used to be. As we have explained, the double-standard nations used to equalise the price for the rest of the world, and now it seems probable that they will do so no longer. An element of uncertainty would thus be introduced into the largest international operations of the United States, which might be very important, and which it is difficult to estimate beforehand. But in all likelihood this uncertainty would not be so great as that caused by the inconvertible and ever-fluctuating greenbacks which the United States have now borne very patiently for many years.

Thirdly—The United States will, by choosing silver for their money, undoubtedly suffer by using the less convenient metal for large transactions instead of the more convenient. Silver is bulky to carry, and cumbersome to count. But a good and secure system of paper money might easily be devised, which would reduce this disadvantage to minor proportions; though that system, like all systems of paper money, is liable to the objection that it may be at any moment departed from, and a bad paper money substituted for a good. No nation which is engaged in first-rate commerce should select a silver money, unless it believes that its circumstances, the character of its people, and the peculiarities of its Government enable it to manage a paper one.

The great reason for inquiring whether it would not be best for the United States to take silver as a money, and not gold, is that it is much more likely to be done. It is always a great advantage to have a strong private interest concurring with and enforcing a great national interest. And here the silver-producers are anxious to sell their silver, and fearful that they may not be able to do so. Whereas the gold-producers, on the other hand, feel sure of their market, and are careless what happens. The fear is that the United States may go on for many years to come with inconvertible paper, as they have for many years past; the difficulties of resuming specie payment are very considerable, and when resumed it may not be kept to unless it is some one's interest that it should be so. But the silver-producers are clearly strong in Congress, wish to get their silver substituted for greenbacks, and would be watchful to see that owing to keeping too small a reserve or other mismanagement, greenbacks did not come back again, if they had once been got rid of. And these producers can put the argument in a way very attractive to American nationalism. They can say, "If you use silver you will raise its value, not only here, but throughout the civilised world. You will support an interest which needs supporting, and you will hurt no one, but make America richer by so doing." And all nations—especially nations which govern themselves—are apt to be much moved by such reasoning.

We hope, therefore, that the American Commission will not be distracted by the old phases of the currency question, and that they will give their attention to the new points presented by the present new relation between gold and silver, and the respective advantages and disadvantages of the courses they have to choose from. There is not one of them which has not much of both, and, in such case, only very deliberate study can show how to bring out the most good with the least evil.

XII.

THE PERMANENT EFFECT OF AN INCREASE OF "COUNCIL BILLS" ON THE FLOW OF SILVER TO INDIA AND UPON THE INDIAN EXCHANGES.

[FROM THE "ECONOMIST" OF OCTOBER 7, 1876.]

THE depreciation of silver and its effect on the Indian exchanges have been much discussed, and with the best result. The Indian Government, we are glad to say, have announced that they would adhere to right principles, notwithstanding the greatness and suddenness of the difficulty in which they are placed, and the number of wrong schemes obtruded upon them. But another fact, of which the practical effects are inextricably intermingled with those of this depreciation,—the recent great increase of the political payment of tribute which England derives from India,—has not been studied with equal care. It appears from the investigations of Mr. Goschen's Committee that the "Indian Council" bills, which represent that payment, have increased in the last ten years as follows:—

Year.	Bills of Exchange Drawn on India.
1865-66	£6,998,899
1866-67	5,613,746
1867-68	4,137,285
1868-69	3,705,741
1869-70	6,980,122
1870-71	8,443,509
1871-72	10,310,339
1872-73	13,939,095
1873-74	13,285,678
1874-75	10,841,615
1875-76	12,389,613

It appears also from the same authority that most of the effect which this great increase in the payment from India to England might be expected to have upon the exchanges, was delayed by a simultaneous increase in the payments made from England to India. Till quite recently we have been very largely investing capital in railways and other public works; the funds necessary for these were raised in London, and were sent out to India; and so compensated for the increase of the tribute. But now there is no longer any equal transmission of capital to India, and we, therefore, for the first time feel the effect of that increase.

The immediate result has naturally been to counteract the flow of silver to the East. When commerce is left to itself, the imports England takes from India are much greater than the imports which India takes from England, and a part of the balance has to be paid for in specie—the rest being settled in indirect ways, of which we need not speak now. But the increase in the "Council bills" provided a competing remittance with silver; if a merchant wanted to make a payment in Calcutta, he had the choice either to buy bills, or send out silver, and of course so much less silver was sent.

The effect was the greater because the Government of India must bring their money home from India, and, therefore, must sell their bills; whereas "silver," like any other commodity, may go to many markets, and may be held when its price falls. This is the reason of the saying, "the price of Council bills rules the price of silver—not the price of silver that of Council bills." It is the price which the more anxious seller must accept that for the moment predominates, and not that which the less anxious can wait for.

So far all is clear, and has been well discussed; but what has not been equally discussed is the question—Will this effect be permanent? How far will the increase of its political payments prevent India from obtaining silver, which is the material of its money? And if it ceases to have this effect, why does it do so?

It clearly cannot have this effect always, or a country like India might be prevented, by an increase in the tribute which she has to pay, from obtaining money altogether. Suppose a dependent country obtains all her supplies of bullion from the dominant country to which she belongs, and that the dominant country imposes an annual tribute equal to the amount of silver which she annually takes—if the consequence of the tribute be to prevent the export of bullion by an equal amount, the dependent country would cease to obtain money altogether, and prices in it would fall and fall indefinitely.

In fact, of course, this will not happen, because as

soon as prices fall below a certain amount an encouragement is given to the export and a discouragement to the import trade, and so a new adverse balance of trade is created, which will take bullion to the dependent country. The effects of the imposition of a tribute on the industry of a dependent country are two: first, to drive away all cosmopolitan capital, which can carry on its business elsewhere. It takes for the use of the Government a certain portion of what used to be the profit of the capitalist, and if in any other country capital does not pay an equal tax, that large class of capitalists who now belong to all countries will go to some other, and will carry on their business there. And secondly, the residential capitalists, whom no motive will tempt away, must be content with a less rate of profit than they used to receive. Particular industries, for which the dependent country has special advantages, will to some extent be an exception, but, as a rule, the effect of the augmented tribute will be to lower prices, because as a rule, and for almost all commodities, it will fix profits on a lower range.

A country which has a tribute to pay of £15,000,000 annually must send abroad annually £15,000,000 worth of commodities more than she receives; the profits of her various industries must be less by that £15,000,000; prices must be lessened to effect this; and (supposing, as is the case with India, that this country does not produce the precious metals) prices will be thus lessened by a corresponding reduction in the import of those metals.

Thus, in the case of India, the effect of her augmented political payments will be to lower the level of prices, till her exports rise above her imports by an equal sum. Till that level is reached, silver will not be sent from England, but when it is reached silver will be sent at once. The effect of the augmentation, therefore, is not to lessen the export of silver from England to India permanently, but only to diminish it temporarily and till the course of commerce has adapted itself to the new circumstances. India will not, indeed, receive *quite* as much as before the increase of her tribute; she will have a somewhat smaller stock of silver to maintain, in order to carry on her trade, as prices are lower (which means that less silver does the same work), and, therefore, the annual supply requisite to maintain prices at that level will be less. But this is but a very minor effect, which is not of much practical account, and, except so far as its influence extends, the import of silver into India will eventually be as much, now that Council bills are £15,000,000, as it used to be when they were £5,000,000.

Some persons who have been much in contact with the recent phenomena of the silver market, but who have not considered the more permanent parts of the subject, will probably be surprised at this conclusion, but this is only one of very many instances in which a great familiarity with the momentary facts of a particular kind of business is a wrong, rather than a right guide, as to what the course of that business in the long run will be.

It will be seen that the case of India is a very peculiar one. Not only is she, politically, dependent on England, but she derives her silver from hence, too. The country which imposes the tribute, and thereby tends to take money, is also the country which supplies money. Ordinarily the imposition of a tribute on a subject-country is much simpler in its effects. The dominant and the subject-countries are only connected by the usual trading relations; coin and bullion only pass to settle the balance of trade, and, in the long run, pass about equally both ways. In this case the effect on the flow of bullion is, on the face of it, only temporary. There being no continuous export of bullion from the dominant country to be arrested, the question whether it will or will not be arrested does not arise. The dominant country simply takes a portion of the produce of the industry of the dependent, and so far renders it less profitable. The range of prices in the dependent country must necessarily be lowered to effect this end, and for a time the supply of the precious metals to it will be diminished. But upon its permanent import of those metals the imposition of the tribute will have no effect. As soon as the proper range of prices is reached, the bullion trade will go on as usual. And so it is in the case of India also, though England's being the country which supplies bullion as well as that which imposes the political payment, seems at first to make a difficulty. Substantially the effect of the new tribute will be the same in this case as in all others.

But though the increase of the Council bills will not, as we have thus shown, change the quantity of silver sent to the East, it may have lasting effects on the Indian exchanges, and next week we will examine whether it has or not.

XIII.

THE EFFECT OF THE "COUNCIL BILLS" ON THE INDIAN EXCHANGES.

[FROM THE "ECONOMIST" OF OCTOBER 14, 1876.]

WE proved last week that the effect of the augmentation of the political payment from India to England, shown by the recent increase of the bills drawn by the Indian Council upon India, will have no permanent effect whatever on the export of silver to India. The great influence which it has had in that respect will be transitory only. We have now to see whether the equally great effect which that increase has had on the Indian exchange will be equally temporary.

To simplify the subject, which is complex, let us first take the simple case of a dominant and a subject-country, which have the same currency, whose trade exports usually balance each other, and neither of which produces the precious metals, or depends on the other for the supply of the precious metals. In this case, there being only one currency in the two countries, the quotations of exchange will be always made in their most intelligible form, that is, by the premium or discount on the bills which each country draws on the other. In this case, bills on the dominant country in the dependent, and bills on the dependent in the dominant, will, as a rule, be equally often at a premium. The trade exports from the ruler to the subject exactly equal those from the subject to the ruler; the bills generated by them will, therefore, be equal, and also the demand for means of remittance. There is no indebtedness between the countries to be settled, and so, on the average, everything will be even between them.

If this state of things is disturbed by the imposition of a tribute, the first effect is that bills in the dependency on its superior rise to a premium; that tribute has to be paid, and these bills are inquired for as the best means of payment. It becomes more difficult (as Indians would say) to "remit home," because there is more to be remitted, and no increase in the means of remittance. The premium will probably rise above the specie point, and coin or bullion will be temporarily sent to the dominant country in consequence. But it can only be so sent temporarily, for the dependency we are considering does not produce the precious metals. In time, therefore, some other means of payment must be found; the tribute must be paid not in gold or silver, but in other commodities. These commodities will begin to be exported as soon as that export becomes profitable; and that profit will consist of two elements—first, of the difference between the price of the commodities in the dominant country and the price in the dependency; and secondly, of the premium at which the merchant in the dependency can sell his bill. The imposition of the tribute will have caused both elements of profit. By producing an export of specie from the dependency, it will have lowered prices there; and by creating a demand for the means of remittance, it will have raised the price of the bills. There will, so to say, be a *bounty* on export caused by the state of the exchange, and the export will be made when the price-profit, *plus* that bounty, are together up to the rate which the capitalist wants. Before that the export will not take place, but after that it immediately will.

And this state of prices and of the exchange will, except other causes interfere with it, tend to be permanent. There is nothing in the relation of the dominant and inferior country to alter either. Till the whole tribute is paid both will, as a rule, continue in this condition, and if the tribute is an annual payment, every year the same causes will be at work, and the same consequences will happen. The profit on the sale of the bill will more or less help the price-profit, and cause the operation to be made earlier than it would if the price-profit only could be obtained.

The effect of this is to enable the dependency to "get off," so to speak, and pay its tribute with a less alteration in the level of its prices than would otherwise have been necessary. In so far as the payment of the tribute is aided by the state of the exchange, it is in fact aided by a *loan*. The seller of the bill gains funds from the money market, which return to that market when that bill is paid. As the transaction is a continual one, always being renewed, the final result is that the dependency pays a part of its annual tribute by a chronic floating debt, which the exporters of its commodities borrow, and from which it derives the benefit. And it will make no matter if the exports are shipped not directly to the dominant country, but to some third country, to which the dominant country owes money. In the latter case, the country which receives the exports from the dependency pays for them by a draft on the dominant country, and that draft is taken as a payment of the tribute. The dependency pays the debt of the ruling country, and this is quite as good as the direct export of value to it.

And no part of this will in the least be altered by the fact that the two countries, the dominant and the dependent, use different currencies, if these currencies are both of the same metal, whether gold or silver. The mode of expressing the exchange by the equation between the coins is only a complex way of expressing the premium and the discount on bills at the moment. Two calculations have in such a case necessarily to be made in buying and selling a bill; the currency of one country has to be turned into that of the other, and the premium or discount of the bill to be ascertained. And for convenience' sake, in the common mode of quoting the exchange, the two computations are put together, and their joint effect told. But there may be a real temporary difference, if the currencies are of different metals. If the metal of the currency in which the relative tribute is fixed falls in value, the tribute is lightened, and if it rises, the tribute is made heavier. And this will affect prices and the exchange, just as an increase or decrease of the tribute in any other way. But the principle of the argument is unaffected.

Nor is that principle really changed if the dependency, like India, receives its supplies of the precious metals, that is, of money, from the dominant country.

In that case, before the tribute is enforced, the exports from the dependency to or on account of the dominant country will be greater than its imports from it. Bills in the dependency drawn on the dominant country will be in general at a discount, and those drawn in the dominant country at a premium. There will be a greater facility of remitting money from the inferior to the superior country than, *vice versâ*, from the superior to the inferior. And therefore, when the tribute is imposed, the new demand for remittance, so created in the inferior country, will have "some lee-way" to make up. Finding bills at a discount, it will have to go on till it makes them at a premium. It will have to stop the flow of specie to the dependency, and if this is not enough to reduce prices, it must go on till it turns the tide the other way, and sends bullion, contrary to its natural course, back from the dependent to the dominant country. But it cannot permanently have this effect because, as we have seen, the supplies of bullion will in the long-run be the same after the imposition of the tribute as before it. The exchange will settle down so that the usual amount of bullion will pass. But subject to this, the consequences will be the same as before. Bills in the dependencies will not be so often or so much at a discount as they would otherwise have been, or bills in the dominant country so often or so much at a premium. And the exports from the dependency, which used to be depressed by that discount, will be less depressed, and the exports from the superior country, which used to be encouraged by that premium, will be less encouraged. But the final effect will be the same; the adjustment of prices and the adjustment of the average exchange taken together will be such as to cause the imports from the dependency to the dominant country to exceed, by the extent of the tribute, those from the dominant country to the dependency (specie included). The tribute will be paid in an excess of value consigned from the dependency to or on account of the dominant country above that consigned the contrary way. In so far as that result is attained by a change in the premium on bills, and not by a change of prices, the dependency is enabled, in this case as before, to pay its tribute by an exportation of fewer commodities than it would otherwise have to export. It obtains a loan to that extent from the money market, just in the same way and just with the same effect as before.

The last case we have been considering is that of India exactly, and it therefore appears that though the increase of the "Council bills" will have no permanent effect on the export of silver to the East, yet it will have a considerable effect on the value of the rupee as quoted for exchange, and that it will tend to make remittances from England to India easier, and from India to England less easy, as long as it continues.

XIV.

THE MINUTE OF THE INDIAN GOVERNMENT ON THE DEPRECIATION OF SILVER.

[From the "Economist" of October 28, 1876.]

The Minute in which the Government of India have replied to the petition of the Bengal Chamber of Commerce that they would suspend the coinage of silver for private persons is a very able document. It shows with admirable clearness that the effect of the plan proposed by the Chamber would be to give the rupee an artificial value, to lower prices, and to disorder trade. It observes that "it is essential to a sound system of currency that it be automatic. No man, or body of men, can ascertain whether, at any particular moment, the interests of the community, as a whole, require an increase or diminution of the currency; still less, how much increase or how much decrease is, at any moment, exactly needed. No Government which aspires to keep its currency in a sound condition would be justified in attempting that impossible task; or, in leaving the community, even for a short interval, without a fixed metallic standard of value. Under an 'open-coinage system,' these things regulate themselves without official interference."

And on this ground it declines to become the sole

coiner of rupees in India, and says that the amount of the silver coinage must be left as before, to the action of the Indian people, who are the best judges of their own wants.

The Minute shows also by a careful review of all the circumstances, that there is, at any rate as yet, no reason for a change in the Indian currency, as no one can yet say what will be the value of silver, either as compared with gold or with commodities. As has been abundantly proved in this country, no action in the matter is at present required of the Government of India, and by far the preponderant probability is that no action will ever be required of it.

The newest, and to us the most interesting, part of the Minute is that which is devoted to explaining that, in the judgment of the Indian Government, it is not yet proved that there is any depreciation at all, certainly not a depreciation to the extent which is commonly believed:—"The divergence now noticeable in the values of gold and silver does not necessarily prove a diminution in the value of silver. It may be equally well accounted for by a rise in the value of gold; and, in fact, it is probable that, since the commencement of this divergence in November, 1872, there has been an increase in the value of gold as well as a decrease in the value of silver. The actual values, measured in silver, of general commodities, whether in India or in England, afford, as yet, no evidence of any recent, sudden, or violent fall in the value of silver; and, if *a priori* considerations strongly indicate that silver must have fallen, such considerations also make it probable that gold must have risen in value. Appended to this resolution is a series of tables of prices in London and in India, the information contained in which points to two conclusions :—First, that gold has risen in value since March, 1873, and especially since last December.* Secondly, that it is not shown that silver has fallen in value, *i.e.*, as compared with commodities in general, either in London or in India, during the same period. These conclusions are open to correction on a wider review of the economical causes which have been at work during the period; but they appear to indicate a rise in the value of gold as at least one of the causes which have disturbed the equilibrium of the two metals. The bearing of both conclusions upon the questions now before the Government of India is important."

As far as gold is concerned, the tables which are given by the Government are ostensibly those which we have often laid before our readers. It is undeniably true that the gold-prices of commodities are, as a rule, less in 1876 than they were in 1873. And in this sense it is true that gold has appreciated, as against commodities. But then it is equally true, and equally shown by the figures of the Minute, that the gold-prices of commodities were more in 1873 than they were in 1869 or 1870. And if we are to say that gold is *ap*preciated now as against 1873, we must, by parity of reasoning, say that it was *de*preciated in 1873 as against 1869. In fact, as all our readers are aware, 1873 was the culminating point of one of the rising periods of price, just as 1869 was the lowest point of the falling period. We wrote on the subject at the time,—on the 4th January, 1873 :—

"The main cause of these cycles in price and trade

* *i.e.*, December, 1875.

is, as we have often shown, the different amounts of loanable capital which are available at different times for the supply of trade. After great panics like 1847, 1857, and 1866, for a very long period enterprise is so slack and credit so bad, that there is no possibility of employing an increasing capital to advantage. Trade continues much as it was, whereas the savings of the country are accumulating constantly. Accordingly there is at such seasons a constant excess in the supply of loanable capital over good bills and other accredited securities; the rate of interest, which is the barometer of the relative supply of these articles, continues very low generally through a series of years. After a certain period some circumstance more or less powerful occurs to augment trade; and then the effect of that capital is felt. Enterprise revives as credit grows, and that capital is lent largely. Till some stimulating event happens, experience shows that such capital may lie almost idle, and that in consequence for years the rate of interest may continue long very low. Bankers—the principal holders of that capital—do not and cannot manufacture securities; they remain quiet and passive till securities of what they consider a substantial kind are offered to them. But when from some cause peculiar to itself trade does revive, bankers are only too eager to lend, and trade, so far from wanting the money which it requires, finds the accumulated capital of bankers lying ready and waiting to be used by it. The development of one trade, too, is never isolated. If any one great industry—say the iron trade—starts into sudden prosperity, the purchasing power of all persons connected with the iron trade is largely augmented, and all the dependent trades, and all the trades in which those concerned in the iron trade lay out their money increasingly, thrive in consequence. And these second and dependent trades quicken other third trades dependent on them, and so on through the industrial world. The first period of every industrial cycle is a period of immense new production, and of great prosperity running through and permeating all trades.

"This period is also one of very high price. The loanable capital—the deposits which have accumulated in the years of depression—are then poured into trade. These have the effect of new money. They are a new purchasing power, which augments all prices dealt in, and especially the prices of wholesale articles, which are those upon which enterprise most acts, and in which speculation is quickest and most constant. Experience shows, too, that the rise in prices so produced is a cardinal element in every investigation of the value of money. The effect of the Australian and Californian gold cannot, as Mr. Jevons was the first to show, be even tolerably investigated unless this periodical cause of elevation in price is first eliminated, and its effects separately set aside."

And in the same way now we must be careful not to confound this sort of appreciation of gold with that which would arise from a diminished production consequent on increased difficulty of attainment. This last would have a tendency to be permanent—at least, to last as long as the increased difficulty of attainment lasted; but the appreciation, which is part of the cycle of prices, is sure not to be permanent; it is only a passing incident in the mercantile world, and is sure to be followed by an equal depression.

It may be said that the present appreciation of gold is due to the new demand for it in Germany and elsewhere. But this demand tells two ways. What we are comparing is the high range of prices in 1873 as compared with the low one in 1876; and one of the effects of the German demand for gold in 1872 and 1873 was to make the rate of discount often much higher in Lombard Street than it would otherwise have been, and so to reduce the prices of all commodities which rise in the speculative times. If it had not been for the German demand for gold, the range of prices in 1873 would have been higher than it was. We cannot, therefore, attribute the fall in prices since 1873 to that demand, for it was then already producing a great effect—a greater, indeed, we think we could show if necessary, than it ever did afterwards.

The gold-price of silver has now been affected in the same way as the gold price of other commodities for the first time, because it has been now for the first time a commodity in the same position as other commodities. Formerly, the existence of a "double standard" in various important countries took off from the market part of any sudden extra supply of gold or silver, replaced it by an equal supply of the other, and so equalised the price. But now that the "equilibrating apparatus" has been withdrawn, the price of silver in gold upon the London market will be affected by the causes which produce cycles of price, just like anything else. How far in this case it has been so affected it is difficult to say, because we have no experience. All commodities are not equally affected by these cycles; some are more so, some less, and we cannot say beforehand what will be the effect on any one. The causes which determine this are too many, and their proportions too unknown, for *a priori* reasoning.

But, as far as we can judge, we should not be disposed to attribute so much effect to this cause as the Indian Government would seem, from the prominence they have given to it, to be inclined to do. So long as silver is largely used as a currency by many countries, it is likely to be a commodity superior to the average of commodities in stable value. All currency commodities, so to speak, are so. Their efficiency in exchange diminishes with any decrease in their value, and a greater quantity of them is required. In no other kind of article does a fall in price generate so large an increase of demand, and therefore so much tend to be its own cure. We should therefore expect silver to be ordinarily much less affected by the causes making "cycles" of price than other commodities.

The figures contained in the table attached to the Minute confirm this view. They show that, taking the prices of each article in March, 1873, as 100, the price of the following articles in the London market was—

Prices in London of Certain Commodities in March, 1873, Compared with April, 1876.

	March, 1873.	April, 1876.
Beef, inferior...	100	110·00
Coffee	100	95·37
Beef, prime small	100	104·76
Silver, bar	100	89·54
Copper, Chili bars	100	88·27
Flour, town made	100	86·17
" New York	...	83·20
Wheat, American red spring, at N. Y.	...	90·06
Wool, South Down hogs	100	80·48

	March, 1873.	April, 1876.
Saltpetre	100 ...	80·18
Cotton, No. 40 mule twist	100 ...	80·35
Wheat	100 ...	81·90
Pepper	100 ...	64·77
Sugar, foreign Muscovado	100 ...	71·79
Cotton, middling uplands	100 ...	68·92
Coals, Hetton Wallsend, London ...	100 ...	63·43
Sugar, Mauritius	100 ...	69·08
Straits tin	100 ...	49·14
Scotch pig iron (warrants)	100 ...	49·19

From this we see that silver has not, in matter of fact, changed as much during the time we are considering as many other articles. And upon the whole, the well known causes tending for the moment to depreciate it—the extra supply from Germany, the want of demand from the "Latin Union," and the apprehension of the new mines—seem to us, as far as we can measure them, causes of a far greater probable effect than the cyclical causes, as far as they affect silver. The utmost we should be inclined to say is, that the cyclical causes produced a weak market, and that the effect of the other causes was in some degree aggravated by this weakness. We believe the special causes affecting silver to be those to which its depreciation is principally owing, and that the causes acting on the value of all commodities only in a minor degree contributed to it.

We are not indeed sure that the Minute was meant to claim for the appreciation of gold more than this subsidiary effect; but the prominent place which is given to it might mislead unwary readers into thinking otherwise. As a whole, both in its conclusions and its reasonings, the "Minute" is most admirable. India is singularly fortunate in having rulers so well able to understand and to cope with a difficulty so peculiar and so little expected.

XV.

A PROPOSED REMEDY FOR THE DEPRECIATION OF THE SILVER COINAGE OF INDIA.

[FROM THE "ECONOMIST" OF NOV. 11, 1876.]

IT has been suggested that the coinage of rupees should be suspended in India; that their importation should be prohibited; that gold should be coined for any one who will take it to the mint at a fixed rate (say at 2s. the rupee); that both rupees and gold should be legal tender, which every one must accept, but that for the present, at least, no one should be able to demand gold. And in this way it is hoped that a gold standard would be introduced into India, without the Indian Government having to buy gold to exchange for silver, the cost of which would be more than it could afford.

But when examined, it will be seen that this is a plan not for introducing into India a gold standard, but a double standard of a peculiar sort. Though the coinage of rupees is suspended, they are still to be legal tender, and their value will therefore continually rise; they will be "monopoly coins," so to speak, circulating at a scarcity value, and they will so circulate concurrently with gold. And this is to be the perpetual currency of India, for the only motive for thinking of it is that silver is already about to fall greatly in value;—its very adoption would for a very long time cause such a fall, because it would close the Indian market against silver—and therefore the cost of buying gold to exchange for the rupee currency of India will be, years hence, more insuperable than it is now.

But to this plan there are the gravest objections. First—a currency of "monopoly coins," circulating much above their cost-value, is sure to cause their forgery. This is as certain as that a high tariff will cause smuggling. If silver should fall enough to make this scheme worth thinking of, the gain by coining rupees in India, or importing them into India, would be very great, and we may depend upon it capital would go into the business. Some of the shrewdest people in the world—the American producers of silver—would have an interest in managing it, and we may be sure they would manage it. The case must not be confounded with that of a "token coinage" of silver such as we have in this country, because our silver coins are only legal tender for small sums, and therefore great masses of them are useless. But in the plan supposed, "monopoly coins" would be the main currency of India, and any quantity of them could be got rid of. India would seem to have most unusual facilities for the operation, for there are native States embedded in our territory where we hardly know what happens, and there is a rich monetary class of shroffs and bankers who would feel no effectual moral scruple against disposing of illicit rupees. The moral objection to such a currency as one of perpetual use is very great, for it is an incessant temptation to diffused fraud, and this evil would be fastened on India for ever.

Secondly—the confusion in trade it would cause would be extreme. Suppose it were now enacted that no more rupees should be coined, and that gold should be coined at 2s. the rupee, the export trade from India, now stimulated by the low exchange, would be stopped, for the exchange would gradually rise; nor for a time at least would the import trade into India find a corresponding gain, for a great uncertainty would be produced, in which no new business would be created, though old business would be stopped.

Thirdly—this would deprive India of the great advantage she will gain, if the present state of things continue, as the *entrepôt* through which silver is introduced into the East. This is always the effect of a lowered value of the currency-metals. The first persons who get them from the mines gain much; those who buy them from the mining people gain much too; and so on, till the depreciation is effected. In the case of India, the importation of silver will gradually raise silver prices; this will bring imports into India from other countries where they have not risen. For very many years England has, in this way, derived the greatest advantage from being the first country to which the Australian gold was sent, and from which it was diffused. The Indian Finance Minister is no doubt troubled by the fall of silver, because he has to buy gold in London, but India itself will probably be benefited by it, for it would give her an easy money market and an extending trade for exports and imports, which the suggested scheme would spoil.

Fourthly—the currency so introduced would be a

very bad one. There would be one currency fit for foreign payments—the gold—and another not so fit. The "monopoly coins" would be unexportable, and so, when any one wanted to make a foreign payment, he would have to get gold, which, as a rule, would make gold at a premium. The effect would be just like that of a plan, often discussed formerly in England, viz., making the notes issued on securities by the Bank of England (the £15,000,000) inconvertible—the rest remaining convertible. The "monopoly" rupees would be of limited number and artificial value, just like the security, or Government notes, we used to discuss, and their effect would be exactly what Lord Overstone predicted, in 1857, in his evidence on Bank Acts:—"Our affairs would then go on very much in the way that a man would walk with one of his legs six inches shorter than the other. One set of notes would circulate at a depreciation compared with the other set of notes; hence great inconvenience and confusion would arise.

"4050. What would be the real effect of it?—The effect would be, that you would have paper money of two different characters in the country, not of equivalent value; not circulating indiscriminately each for all purposes, but some useful for one purpose and some useful for the other, and that there would be intolerable confusion. A man would have Government notes, and he would present them to another man in payment; that man would say, 'I do not want Government notes; I want to make a remittance abroad; I cannot get bullion for those Government notes; I will not take them.'

"4051. Are they both to be a legal tender?—They

would both be a legal tender as far as the Government is concerned, but the Government note would not be a legal tender between individuals.—Then what is that individual to do?—The other man says to him, 'You must go and get me the other notes. Either you or I must pay a premium for them.'

"4052. What would be the harm of that?—The harm would be, enormous injustice and intolerable confusion."

In the plan now suggested—monopoly coins being compulsory tender—gold not being demandable,—it would be settled which party should pay the "premium." Everybody would be obliged to take the purely domestic medium of exchange, and to buy with it the medium which is also of foreign use. But in other respects the evil would be exactly what Lord Overstone describes. There would be two currencies in the country with different values, and prices in one would, as far as the discrepancy went, be different from those in the other.

For a short time, and during a period of transition, we can quite imagine that this inconvenience might be endured. But the present plan is by its essence a permanent plan—a plan for making a currency for India for all time; and then an inherent effect of great magnitude such as this becomes a most grave objection. As Lord Overstone said of the old plan—"Then, you would have a certain proportion of the monetary system of the country circulating at a discount; I cannot conceive a greater state of monetary disorganisation than that."

No doubt, it is said, that the Indian Government may "regulate" the currency; that it may withdraw rupees from circulation; that it may add to the gold in circulation, and so equalise the value of rupees and gold. But to succeed in such an attempt, the Indian Government would want to know the amount of currency required for foreign payments, which is that which causes the difference between silver and gold; and this they never could know. And American experience of "gold sales" and greenback withdrawals is a great warning against giving any Government the power of arranging the currency. It is sure to injure the good repute if not the real good faith of the Government (for it necessarily creates pecuniary secrets of great value), and, nevertheless, it is not at all sure to attain its end, and to equalise, as is intended, the two kinds of currency.

For these reasons, we cannot think that the suggested plan for a new Indian currency would be a good one, even if it could be shown that silver was sure to be permanently excessively depreciated. And as the preponderating probability seems at present to be, that it will *not* be so depreciated, we are still more of opinion that it would be unwise to begin a policy on the face of it, and almost admittedly, so anomalous.

XVI.

THE TRANSITION STATE OF THE SILVER MARKET.

[From the "Economist" of December 9, 1876.]

The delicacy of the silver market at present is curiously illustrated by the course of the price of silver in the London Market this year. First, there was an immense fall, and now there has been an equivalent rise. The figures are—

				d.		d.
In 1876 the fluctuations in	January	were between	...	$56\frac{1}{8}$	and	$54\frac{7}{8}$
" "	February	"	...	$54\frac{7}{8}$	"	53
" "	March	"	...	$54\frac{1}{4}$	"	$52\frac{1}{2}$
" "	April	"	...	54	"	$53\frac{1}{2}$
" "	May	"	...	54	"	52
" "	June	"	...	52	"	50
" "	July	"	...	$51\frac{1}{2}$	"	$46\frac{3}{4}$
" "	August	"	...	$53\frac{3}{4}$	"	50
" "	September	"	...	$52\frac{9}{16}$	"	$51\frac{1}{8}$
" "	October	"	...	$53\frac{1}{2}$	"	52
" "	November	"	...	55	"	$53\frac{1}{8}$

Present price, December 10th, $56\frac{1}{4}$d.

Such rapid changes of so great a magnitude could only happen in a very delicate market, where a little extra supply, or even only an apprehension of an extra supply, will at once send down prices, and where a slight extra demand, especially when it seems at all likely to be permanent, will at once send them up. The delicacy in this case has been due to the fact that the silver market is now in an entirely new state, and that until the conditions which regulate that state are discovered, all dealers are fearful of keeping any considerable amount on hand. They sell what comes as it comes, which sends down the price; and in consequence they have none to sell when there is a sudden demand for an extra quantity, and therefore the price rises.

In former times it was not necessary to keep a stock of silver, and there was no motive for it, for the "Latin Union," being a collection of countries with a double standard, held an immense stock for all the world. If silver showed a tendency to rise in price, gold immediately was sent to purchase it in the country where it could be obtained at a fixed price in gold. And similarly, any stock of silver which accumulated here was carried off to the "Latin Union" as soon as it had the least tendency to depress the price. Much silver could not be kept in stock, and there was no motive for keeping any. But now this peculiar organisation has ceased to act, for the "Latin Union" has practically ceased to be a "double standard" league, because it does not coin, and therefore does not take new silver in indefinite amounts when required.

The silver market will therefore in future, like all other markets, have to secure its stability by keeping a "stock on hand." Dealers will hold for what they think a good price, which will usually prevent an extreme fall of price, and get rid of more or less of this accumulation when there is an unusual demand, which will commonly prevent an extreme rise. But a great number of causes as yet prevent the dealers from doing so. First, the uncertain quantity which the German Government may at any time sell hangs over the market; the effect of the increase of the "Council bills" on the Indian demand for silver has still to be fully tested in practice—indeed, it will require years so to test it; the American production is still an unknown quantity, though everything seems to show that it will be much less than it was thought to be; the "Latin Union" is still in an "expectant attitude," and may possibly resume its old policy. Till these causes have ceased to operate as powerfully as they now do, no important stock of silver will be kept, since the future is too uncertain to justify it, and until it is kept the price will probably fluctuate a good deal, though not as much as during the past year, when most of the influences that cause variation have been at a maximum, and most of those which cause stability at a minimum.

The rise in the price of silver which has just taken place is as local as the fall which preceded it. The great mass of prices in the countries using silver as a money are wholly unaffected by it. Indeed, such perturbations as a rise of 20 per cent., and then a fall to the old level, during a single year in the general prices of great countries, would have been economical phenomena such as the world has never seen, and such as would have caused a vast derangement of transactions.

The silver market must settle down into its normal condition before we shall know what will be the normal price of silver in relation to gold or to commodities. The disturbing forces with which we have had so long to deal must first pass away. And until they have so passed, it will be desirable that no Government shall involve itself in a currency change, depending on the mutual relations of silver and gold, which has not begun one already. Unless in case of vital necessity, such currency changes should be made at the time when the circumstances attendant on them can be best foreseen, and that is when the course of trade is most regular, and the chief markets in the matter most in their normal condition.

XVII.

BI-METALLISM.

[FROM THE "ECONOMIST" OF DECEMBER 30, 1876.]

WE have written much this year on the subject of silver, and on the evils of its depreciation, but we have hardly, we think, referred to the scheme which some persons think would set right everything—the scheme of universal "bi-metallism." But the truth is, that we regard that scheme as so entirely beyond the boundaries of practical finance that we did not think it worth discussing, and we only discuss it now because we continue to receive ingenious pamphlets, some of them written by men of business, which maintain that it is both practicable and advisable. We shall, therefore, state as shortly as possible our reasons for thinking that it is neither.

The plan is, that by means of an "international conference," or otherwise, all nations should agree to use both gold and silver as legal tender for all amounts, and to use them in the same proportions; which, it is said, would cure any evils which now arise from changes in the relative value of gold and silver, and in the cost of production of both or either of them.

But first, any such attempt would be such an alteration in the monetary system of most countries, that it would be difficult to get most of them to take it into consideration, and impossible to induce many of them to agree to it. Take our own case,—England has a currency now resting solely on the gold standard, which exactly suits her wants, which is known throughout the civilised world as hers, and which is most closely united to all her mercantile and banking habits. What motive, that an English Parliament could ever be got to understand, is there that would induce them to alter it? You cannot even begin an argument which would seem to have a sufficiently striking sound. Some time ago it was indeed said that the finances of our Indian Empire were thrown into confusion by the fall in the price of silver, and that, therefore, the English and the Indian currency should be assimilated, and both be on the "double standard" principle. But even in that case the English people would, rightly or wrongly, never have consented to change their currency; they would have told the Indian financiers to adjust their system of raising a revenue to the new circumstances. They would not have altered the sovereign for anything which might happen to the rupee.

And still less would the English people think of doing so when silver has risen in price, and when our Indian finance is no longer inconvenienced. They would say, with their usual untheoretical common-sense, "This event shows how dangerous it is to make great changes upon fine arguments in important matters. You—the advocates of bi-metallism—wanted us to make a most troublesome and difficult change to cure our evil, which has now for a time entirely, and perhaps for ever, cured itself. We certainly shall be cautious how we listen to you again."

Then it is said that under our present system the fall in silver throws exchanges into confusion, which, no doubt, alters the course of trade. But practical commerce soon adapts itself to such changes, and a nation which at present has a good currency, and one which suits it, would be very foolish to make a change merely to keep the exchanges from possible fluctuation. And as we have often shown before, the fluctuations in the Indian exchange, which have hampered our export trade to India, are not by any means wholly due to the change in the price of silver; they are partly owing to the increase in remittances from the East for interest of debt, and on other accounts; the effect of which was long suspended, but now is fully felt. And, as we have also often shown, though the trade *to* India is impeded by a fall of silver, our trade *from* India—our imports from thence—are stimulated. The same cause which tends to impair the one, tends equally and necessarily to add to the other. A change in the monetary system of any one country can rarely be effected, except to prevent some great evil; a change of the system of a very large number of countries could only be made to meet some superlative evil, and in this case neither exists.

Most advocates of "bi-metallism" now admit that unless all countries adopt it, and unless all countries keep to it, it is a very faulty system. It is not a currency of two metals, but an alternative currency, sometimes of one and sometimes of another. Countries with such an alternative currency always use the cheaper metal and sell the dearer metal. Creditors in it are always injured by being paid in the cheaper metal; debtors are always benefited by being enabled to pay in it. The currency of France was thus a few years ago changed from gold to silver, and would now have been changed back again to gold, if it had not refused to take the silver, and had not, in so doing, practically abandoned the bi-metallic system. And a system which requires that every one should agree to make it good, is certainly a system which is difficult to make good, and which is always liable to become bad.

And even if this system was at once, say, by "miracle," imposed on all the human race, it would be very imperfect. It forces an arbitrary equation, in which there is no naturalness, between gold and silver. But their natural relative price has varied exceedingly. The following table, published by Mr. Goschen's Committee, shows this clearly :—

Date.	Ratio.	Authority.
A.D.		
1526	11·30	Apparent relation of market value as deduced from the British Mint regulations, some absurd and unsuccessful experiments in coinage being disregarded.
1543	11·10	
1561	11·70	French Mint regulations.
1575	11·68	
1551	11·17	German Imperial Mint regulations.
1559	11·44	
1604	12·10	British Mint regulations ; experiments disregarded.
1612	13·30	
1619	13·35	
1623	11·74	Upper German regulations.
1640	13·51	French Mint regulations.
1665	15·10	
1667	14·15	Upper German regulations.
1669	15·11	
1670	14·50	British regulations.
1679	15·00	French regulations.
1680	15·40	
1687—1700	14·97	Ratios calculated from the bi-weekly quotations of the Hamburg prices-current, giving the value of the gold ducats of Holland in silver thalers, down to 1771, and after that in fine silver bars. The nominal par of exchange during this period was 1 : 14·80, and the quotations show the variations of the market-rate in percentage above or below this. At par, six silver marks-banco were equivalent to one ducat, $68\frac{20}{47}$ ducats containing one mark (weight) of fine gold, and $27\frac{3}{4}$ silver marks-banco, containing one mark (weight) of fine silver. Hence, 6 multiplied by $68\frac{20}{47}$, divided by $27\frac{3}{4}$, equals 14·80, the par ratio.
1701—1720	15·21	
1721—1740	15·08	
1741—1790	14·74	
1791—1800	15·42	
1801—1810	15·61	
1811—1820	15·51	
1821—1830	15·80	
1831—1840	15·67	
1841—1850	15·83	

And the effect of the bi-metallic system, if universal, would be to fill the world with the cheaper metal only. That which could be brought to market most easily would come to market; that which could least easily be brought to market would not come. And there would, in consequence, be an incessant tendency to change of prices. No doubt that tendency would be impeded by the magnitude of the stock of the precious metals which now exists, and of which it would have to change the value. But still it would exist, and would be a constant evil.

But this and other characteristics, whether for good or evil, which may belong to universal bi-metallism are, in our judgment, scarcely worth considering; they seem to us fit only for theoretical books, because the plan is only a theory on paper, and will never be in practice tried.

APPENDIX.

APPENDIX.

EVIDENCE BEFORE THE SELECT COMMITTEE ON DEPRECIATION OF SILVER.

MONDAY, 8TH MAY, 1876.

MEMBERS PRESENT:

Mr. Baxter.
Mr. Cave.
Mr. Christopher Beckett Denison.
Mr. Fawcett.
Mr. Goschen.
Lord George Hamilton.
Mr. Hermon.
Mr. Kirkman Hodgson.
Mr. Hubbard.
Mr. Massey.
Sir Charles Mills.
Mr. Shaw.

The Right Hon. George Joachim Goschen, *in the Chair.*

Mr. Walter Bagehot, *called in; and Examined.*

Chairman.

1361. You have been for many years, I believe, the Editor of the *Economist* ?—Yes.

1362. I think you have given particular attention to this Silver question ?—Yes.

1363. Have you considered the relation between the depreciation of silver and the Indian exchanges ?—I have devoted a certain amount of attention to it, and it appears to me to be almost certain that the first immediate effect of the depreciation of silver will be to cause an unfavourable balance of trade with the East; and, in conquence, a great export of silver to the East.

1364. It has been alleged that the depression of the Indian trade has in part contributed already to the depreciation of silver?—I should hardly like to give an opinion on such a point without reading the evidence which has been given before this Committee, which I understand has on this head been contradictory; it appears to me that, to a great extent, the depression in the trade has been common both to exports and imports; and, therefore, would not affect the balance of trade, or, in consequence, the exportation of silver to the East.

1365. If the fall in the value of the crops exported from India to England had been compensated by a corresponding diminution in the exports from England to India, trade might be depressed, but the price of silver would remain unaffected?—Quite unaffected, as far as that goes.

1366. Do you share in the view that has been expressed that the drafts of the Council of India have contributed considerably to the depreciation of silver?—I should rather put it in this way, that the drafts in India represent an increase in the tribute, a beneficial tribute no doubt, which India pays to this country, and, of course, that being a payment which she has to make, alters the exchange, tends to make it unnecessary to remit silver from this country, and, therefore, diminishes the demand for silver.

1367. Do you believe that the fall in the price of silver has operated unfavourably, or is calculated to operate unfavourably, on Indian trade, either temporarily or permanently?—I should say that the effect of the depreciation of silver was to cause an increased export of goods from India to this country, a diminished export from this country to India, and, in that manner, to cause an unfavourable balance of trade.

1368. Could you explain that a little more fully to the Committee?—I think the increase of the export of goods from India to this country will arise in this way: a merchant in London, who is thinking of importing goods from the East, looks at the price current in Calcutta, and he sees the price quoted in rupees. The merchant in London is in possession of sovereigns in London, therefore he has two operations; first, he has to buy his rupees in India; next, with those rupees he has to buy the article which he saw in the price current. The question of profit and loss to him is compounded of the result of those two operations; if, therefore, he can buy his rupees in Calcutta on more favourable terms, he will find it to his interest to go into a speculation which would not otherwise be profitable. If he can get rupees at 1s. 8d. instead of 2s., and he can buy his goods in Calcutta with the same number of rupees, that is so much extra gain to him. Conversely, the English exporter of goods to the East will receive payment in rupees, and he will have to sell those rupees; and if he sells them for a less amount of sovereigns, he will suffer a loss, and that is a discouragement to exporting from this country to India. The result of these two operations, of the encouragement of exports from India to this country, and the discouragement of exports from hence to India, necessarily is an increase of the balance which this country has to pay to India, and consequently a flow of silver to the East.

1369. And is, so far, a counterbalancing element tending to raise the price of silver as compared with the other causes which have been mentioned, which might depress the price of silver?—Quite so; and I should say a cause of even greater magnitude than any which tend to depress it.

1370. It is a rectifying cause?—A rectifying cause, and a rectifying cause of the first magnitude, because what I have said extends not only to India, but to all countries which have a silver currency. Those countries are the great majority of the world; the circulation of silver in those countries is something enormous, and to all those countries you will have to send a certain amount, if the depreciation of silver continues. The quotations of prices in all those countries are made in silver. Traders with those countries have to go through the operation both ways, as to exports and imports, which I have described, in silver. As to all those countries, there will be a bounty on exporting from them, and a discouragement to importing into them, and in consequence to every one of those there will be a flow of silver.

1371. In order that the Committee may thoroughly possess themselves of those particular points, do I understand you correctly that the operation is as follows: a depreciation of silver in India and the depreciation of the Indian exchange have the following effect, that a London merchant desiring to speculate in Indian produce, will be able with his gold to buy a larger number of rupees; and that if the prices remain stationary in India, he will, having a larger number of rupees, be able to buy the exports of India at a cheaper rate himself, and therefore make a larger profit?—Yes, that is one side of the operation.

1372. And, on the other side, that the exporter of goods from this country to India will realise, if the prices have not risen (which is the same supposition), the same number of rupees in India, but in turning them into gold, he will find that the identical number of rupees will furnish him with a smaller amount of gold in return here for his outlay, and that therefore he will make a less profit?—Yes, that is exactly my meaning.

MR. FAWCETT.

1373. That opinion, though, is based on the supposition, that as the depreciation of silver continues the prices remain stationary, is it not? But very soon after the depreciation commences in those countries, where silver is a standard of currency, the rise in prices will be exactly proportioned to the depreciation of silver?—When it is, of course, the encouragement is withdrawn.

1374. After all, the depreciation of a metal which is chosen for the standard of currency is measured and is marked by the rise in prices; that is what depreciation of money means. If you say that money is depreciated 10 per cent., you mean that prices have risen 10 per cent.?—I do not quite understand the question you ask.

1375. If gold were depreciated in this country 10 per cent., it means that gold possesses 10 per cent. less purchasing value?—Yes.

1376. Or, in other words, prices had risen to that extent?—Yes.

1377. The same way in India, where silver, not gold, is the currency, if silver is depreciated to a certain extent, prices must rise to the same extent, therefore, your reasoning is based on an hypothesis which cannot take place in actual life?—No; I consider that it is based on the present facts. The purchasing power of gold over silver by the English merchants is at this moment increased; gold will buy a great deal more silver than it used to do; but the silver prices of articles in Calcutta have not been affected. Silver is not, as yet, depreciated in the East. It is only during the process of depreciation that my argument holds.

CHAIRMAN.

1378. When I asked you your opinion, I drew a distinction between a temporary effect and a permanent effect; the opinion you have stated, I understand you to mean is, the temporary and first effect?—Yes; as soon as the depreciation of silver, as respects the Indian commodities, is equal to its depreciation as respects the gold of the English merchant, then the process which I have described is at an end.

MR. FAWCETT.

1379. What I understand is this, that for a time, it may be shorter or longer, during which the depreciation of silver may take place without affecting general prices, you have indicated the prices which will exercise an influence to restore the value of silver to its former level of value?—The point I wish to make before the Committee is this, that all over the East the process I have described will go on, and that to depreciate silver 2 per cent. all over the East will require a vast amount of silver currency, because the region is so large. No doubt it will stop when the depreciation of 2 per cent., or whatever it may be, has been effected, but that will take a long time.

CHAIRMAN.

1380. The first operation is such as you have described; the next operation would probably be, would it not, that the prices of commodities in India would rise?—Yes.

1381. While silver had been depreciated?—Yes.

1382. Then in proportion as the price of silver rose you would require a larger amount of silver to do the work than had been used before?—Yes.

1383. That increasing need for silver to pay for the aggregate increase due to the rise in prices would be spread over a vast surface, in your opinion?—Yes, that is my meaning.

1384. Namely, over the countries with the silver valuation in the East generally?—Yes.

1385. The greater demand for silver during this process would tend to arrest the fall of silver, *pro tanto*, in your opinion?—That would be a main cause, supposing other causes which tend to depreciate silver to have the effect which is supposed.

1386. In the first instance prices might remain stationary for a short time; then the flow of silver would take place to the country, owing to the encouragement to export and the discouragement of import.—Yes.

1387. And when that was past, and prices rose to their level, so that there was neither that encouragement nor discouragement, the aggregate amount of silver needed for the commerce of those countries would have been increased?—Yes.

1388. After a rise of price all over the East, due to the depreciation of silver, more silver would be required for carrying on the general trade of those countries than before?—Yes; to a very great extent.

1389. Have you at all calculated the surface covered by what is called the silver valuation, as compared with that which is covered by the gold valuation?—It used to be said until a few years ago, that England and Portugal were the only countries where gold was the standard of value; and there were certain countries which had a double standard, but those were not very many; and all the rest were silver. Silver is the normal currency of the world, and from a natural cause, because silver is a much cheaper metal, and is suited to those small transactions which constitute the bulk of the dealings of mankind.

1390. Have you examined the statistics which are available to the public with regard to the aggregate amount of silver and gold in various countries?—I have examined them, but I regret to say that I do not think they are of such value as to be made the basis of sound reasoning in such investigations as this. It appears to me that you neither know with certainty the present stock of silver in the world, nor are you able to estimate the probable augmentation of it; nor do you know the effect which any given per-centage, say 10 per cent. on the stock, would have upon its value. The last part is a matter which has not even been discussed, I think.

1391. You would question, after all the study you have given to the subject, both the accuracy and the real substantial value of figures that go into the aggregate amount of silver and gold in the world, and the proportions of the metals to each other?—I do not believe they are worth the paper on which they are written. I do not consider that any one knows anything about them, or has the means of knowing.

1392. To resume the point of the effect of the depreciation of silver on the Indian exchanges, which is one point referred to this Committee, can you treat that question as one of exports and imports between India and this country alone; I have heard a remark with regard to the effect upon other countries?—Of course it will be evident that if this country has to export silver to the East, it must buy that silver somewhere. That silver it will have to buy in

America, and therefore a consequence of the new state of things will be that the English exporters of goods to some parts of the world will be benefited. I do not say the English exporters of goods to America, for probably we shall not pay America directly. The nature of the trade between America and this country is, that America sends us directly a great deal more than we send her, and America buys, in various parts of the world, coffee, and rice, and tea, and a variety of articles, and that the sellers of those articles draw upon England, and so the balance is struck; we shall have to pay America in some way for the silver, and we shall pay her by exporting to the countries from whom she buys some of those articles, and therefore, though it is perfectly true to say that the effect of the depreciation of silver may be unfavourable to the English exporter of goods to the East, yet it will be favourable to another class of English exporters, that is to say, those who pay America.

1393. You mean this, that as the silver is to be produced, and comes to Europe, or when it comes to Europe, it must be paid for by some means?—It comes here, and we must pay for it. We shall pay for it, not to America directly, in all probability, but by exporting goods to various parts of the world where America buys. She buys in Brazil, in Cuba, and in the East, and in France, and all those countries draw drafts upon England, and ultimately the account is settled in commodities.

1394. If America draws more Eastern produce in consequence of producing more silver, and therefore having something to sell which it can turn into commodities abroad, then a certain amount of new purchasing power is given to those countries from which it draws its exports?—Yes.

1395. And that purchasing power they may again avail themselves of in purchasing from this country?—Yes; such are the dimensions of our trade, that ultimately they come to buy of us. We are the great settling-house of the world.

1396. Have you examined the effect of the depreciation of silver upon our trade up to this date?—I cannot say that I have made such an examination of it as I should like to lay before the Committee, especially as I understand that contradictory opinions have been expressed upon it, and I should rather rely on the general principle I have stated, because the facts of a particular year are far more difficult to discover than the general tendencies which operate over a long period of time.

1397. There are so many disturbing causes in any particular year?—Yes; and it is so difficult to get at the precise facts of any particular year. Statements may be made as to depression of particular trades. Well, what does depression mean? The traders will not come and show you their books; you ought to have a comparative statement of their profits in the period at which the depression is said to commence, and at the period of which you are talking. Now no such account is ever given in, and therefore you are dealing with a statement which you have no means of measuring or testing.

1398. Do I understand you rather to question the prolonged depression in the Indian trade?—I do not doubt that there is a great depression in the export trade from this country, and that that arises very largely from the causes of which I have been speaking. The depreciation of silver has necessarily caused discouragement to export to the East; the people who most call themselves the Eastern trade are the exporters to the East.

1399. Unless the manufacturers and producers in our manufacturing districts have got stocks of articles already manufactured for India which they are bound to sell?—No doubt they will have to sell them practically at reduced prices, because they will sell them in rupees, and when they bring these rupees home they will yield less in sterling money.

1400. Still if they are manufactured they would be likely to be exported?—Yes, and perhaps for other reasons. Some part of the export trade, I would not at all say it is true of the Eastern trade, but some amount of trade is carried on by drawing on consignees for the creation of bills, which bills are discounted in this country; and that trade, which is not of a very healthy description, will always go on, whatever the prices may be.

1401. Do I understand you to mean in very general terms that it is difficult to arrest any particular branch of manufacture and export the moment it becomes unprofitable?—Very difficult indeed. In the first place, an amount of fixed capital is sunk in it which has to be moved, and people have formed habits and connections; and such a general cause as I have been speaking of will not operate perhaps for a considerable period of time.

1402. The export trade from this country to another great consuming country might be prolonged sometimes without its being exactly evidence that that export was the result of sound trade and permanent causes?—Quite so, without its being at all a conclusive indication that it was such a trade as ought to be carried on, or such a trade as anybody would begin.

1403. Would the depreciation of silver have this effect, that it would prevent the extension of business or the initiation of new business while alarm was felt as to the uncertainty of returns through the fluctuations in silver, but it would not cause an immediate cessation and diminution of the trade?—Yes, it would have that effect, it would have a gradual tendency in that direction, a tendency to make the export trade to India cease.

1404. Turning to another subject, the evidence before the Committee, I think, has been generally to the effect that the depreciation of silver has been caused by the increased production or the impression produced by the increased production in America, by the demonetisation in Germany, and by the increase of the drafts of the Indian Council; do you agree in the existence of these causes?—I think that those causes are real, but I think a fourth ought to be added to them.

1405. What is that fourth cause?—A number of States which are grouped together in what is called the Latin Union have ceased to coin silver ever since the year 1874 in the same manner which they did before; as the Committee are aware, the Latin Union is a name for five States, France, Belgium, Italy, Switzerland, and Greece, which up to the year 1874 had what they called a double standard, that is to say, silver and gold were tenders for any amount for debts, and the coinage was framed on the relation of $15\frac{1}{2}$ to 1. Up to that time it was open to anybody to go to the French, or any other mints, with silver or gold, as the case might be, and get it coined; the consequence of course was, that the moment metal became depreciated, the holders took it to those mints and had it coined; but in the year 1874 that process was arrested, because those Governments limited the amount of silver which they would coin, and if it had not been for that change of policy, all the silver which is now flooding the London market, and lowering the price, would have been long since in the mints of those countries; it would have released gold from them, and the combined effect of the two operations would have been, that the comparative value of gold and silver would have been very little altered, probably not at all.

1406. Without giving an opinion as to whether they did right or wrong in the steps they have taken, do I understand you to mean that their abstention from purchasing, whereas formerly they were buyers, must be added to the effect of the demonetisation in Germany ?—The operation of the double-standard caused a supply on speculation ; the moment any one of the two metals becomes depreciated there is a motive to any bullion-dealer to take the depreciated metal to the mint, leave it there, have it coined, and with that he can buy the appreciated metal and have a profit ; in that way, in former times, the old silver currency of France was entirely taken away, and gold substituted for it, merely because gold was cheaper ; in the same way now, if the Latin Union continued to coin as before, gold would have been taken away and silver taken back.

1407. Are you aware that the stock of silver in the Bank of France has increased of late years ?—Yes, I am aware that it is now 20 millions or more.

1408. You contend that but for their cessation of coinage a larger figure than that would have accumulated ?—Yes, and gold would have been taken away from them.

1409. To the same amount ?—To an equivalent amount, not only of France, but the Latin Union generally.

1410. There has been once or twice before, has there not, in France, a change from silver to gold and from gold to silver ?—Yes, we were enabled to pay India in silver for the cotton we wanted during the famine, by getting it from the French currency in this way.

1411. Was France at that time drained of a large portion of its silver currency ?—A very large portion. It was the saying in France at that time, "The English have taken away the silver," meaning that we had sent it to India. It was quite true that it was bought up with gold.

1412. Did we pay a premium on silver at the time ?—Gold was much depreciated as against the legal equation, just as silver is now against the legal equation, and therefore it was profitable to send gold to the Mint.

1413. Had the Governments in the Latin Union not curtailed their coinage even before the year 1874 ?—1874 is the first year in which they made a treaty on this subject, I think.

1414. Can you state to the Committee any facts with regard to the legislation as to Holland ?—It appears to me that the difficulty of Holland in this question is far greater than that of any other country, because they have, as England has, an Indian Empire, and they have the same currency in the Indian Empire as they have at home. They are much in the same position that we should be in if we had a rupee currency here, and we thought of demonetising rupees. It has been proposed to demonetise the Dutch dollar, which is the coinage both of Holland and of Java, and of other Dutch possessions, which circulates in the East to an enormous extent.

1415. The Dutch dollar has not yet been demonetised?—It has not, but proposals are constantly being made, and an experimental step was made last year towards its demonetisation.

1416. Was a Bill passed with regard to it?—Yes; but like many experimental measures, it was very complex; I should not like to explain its exact effect; I have had it explained to me in various ways; it was a small Act in itself, and only of importance as an indication of a policy which was to follow.

1417. Was it a temporary Act or a permanent Act?—Temporary.

1418. To cease when?—To cease very soon, I think, but I am not perfectly certain.

1419. As a matter of fact, when that Act ceases, will the Government of Holland have to make up its mind one way or the other again, and to take some measures?—Either to make a change, or leave things as they are; Holland demonetised gold years ago, and has only a silver currency.

1420. As a matter of fact, without expressing any speculative opinion, they have not yet established a gold valuation?—No, they have greater difficulties in going in that direction than any other country.

1421. I have seen it stated in some publications that Holland was one of those countries that adopted the gold valuation?—That is a complete error; many circumstances much impede them in so doing.

1422. Have they been buying silver or gold latterly to your knowledge?—I could not lay the details before the Committee.

Mr. Fawcett.

1423. The Latin Union, or the Latin Convention, continues in operation till 1880, does it not?—Till some date of that kind.

1424. Therefore its policy, which you think has been influential in assisting the depreciation of silver, will continue till the time when it ceases, when the Confederation breaks up?—Not necessarily; it has an annual meeting, by which it determines the amount of silver which it will coin; I should say that in 1874 they had made a cardinal alteration in their policy; the theory of the double standard is that any one should be able to bring his money to the mint and get it coined in any amount, but that was altered.

CHAIRMAN.

1425. What was the original policy of the Latin Union?—It was the policy of the double standard, as it is called, in which both gold and silver circulate, and are legal tenders for any amount, and in which the relation between them was that of $15\frac{1}{2}$ to 1.

1426. What was the object of their combining?—It was, I suppose, partly a political movement on the part of the French Empire to gain an influence in those countries, and partly the natural wish of countries so intimately connected to have the same coinage, and they adopted the French coinage of that time, as being that of the predominant Power.

1427. The Latin Union was not formed with reference at all to the question as between silver and gold?—They simply adopted the French currency of that time.

1428. The policy to suspend the coinage is the common policy that has been adopted by them in the course of their union, but is not one of the principles of their union?—It is contrary to the fundamental principles of their union. They gave up the double standard the moment they allowed their metal to be limited. The cardinal principle was abandoned.

MR. FAWCETT.

1429. Did not they come to some agreement with reference to the coinage of silver, which agreement was to continue in operation till 1880; I think we have had evidence to that effect?—They met annually, and determined the amount of silver which they should coin.

1430. I think Mr. Giffen gave the evidence, but I fancy we have had evidence to this effect, that when they met in 1874, one of their agreements was that they should continue a certain policy with regard to the coinage until 1880, and that they should be bound by that agreement until that year?—They re-vote annually what the amount shall be, and it is open now to the annual meeting to change, and to go back to the double standard pure and simple. In 1874, the amount which they agreed to coin was £4,800,000. In 1875 it was raised to £6,000,000, and now it has gone back to £4,800,000, in 1876. It is divided between the countries.

1431. You say they cardinally changed their policy in 1874 with regard to the coinage of silver, and their policy with regard to the future of course is uncertain ?—Very uncertain. It is a possibility, I do not say that it is a probability, that they might begin to coin silver in unlimited amounts, and that would take the silver off the market.

1432. On the other hand, it is possible that they may continue this policy, which you think has been influential in assisting the depreciation ?—Yes; or they may go further, and demonetise the silver in France. That has been proposed, and that would throw an additional amount of silver on the market.

1433. Their policy one way or the other will have a considerable effect either in promoting the depreciation of silver, or in retarding its depreciation, and that policy with regard to the future is, in your opinion, obscure and uncertain ?—Yes; it will be a force of the first magnitude.

1434. You would not like, at any rate, positively to predict in what direction that force, which you have described as one of the first magnitude, will operate ?—I think there are very great difficulties in the way of demonetising silver in France, and it is certain, I believe, that the present rulers of France wish to preserve what they call an expectant attitude, and to continue the present state of things, only coining limited amounts, but whether they will be able so to continue I do not know.

1435. Do you think that one element in considering what the value of silver is, is this,—that the value of the precious metal, after all, is determined by the same considerations as the value of any other mineral, or any other commodity, and that consequently the cost of producing those metals, or the cost of raising them, must have an important bearing on their future value ?—Undoubtedly.

1436. Therefore, if the cost of producing silver should greatly diminish, that must sooner or later, just in the same way as if the cost of producing any other article greatly diminished, have its effect upon its value ?—That will of course have an effect upon the value, but it will be limited by several considerations; one is, that it is the cost of production under the most difficult circumstances which regulates the price, not the cost of production in those mines of splendid fertility which we hear of, but the cost of production in the least of the old mines which keeps itself at work.

1437. To draw an analogy, if you suddenly discovered in a

country a great tract of fertile land, the immediate effect of that land being discovered, which would enable agricultural produce to be produced cheaper, would not necessarily be to lower the value of agricultural produce if the demand for it keep on increasing, so that it was necessary to keep the comparatively speaking unfertile land in cultivation, which before had been cultivated ?—Quite so.

1438. But if, on the other hand, this fertile land should so add to agricultural produce that the more unproductive sources of supply which had been before worked should be given up, then the cost of producing that produce would diminish ?—Yes.

1439. You think that would apply as an analogy to the value of the precious metals ?—Yes; I think it would be the mine of the least fertility that should keep itself at work that would regulate the price.

1440. You have described to us very clearly what you think will be the effect on the trade of India, if the depreciation of silver continues, but have you considered what its effect on the revenue of India is ?—I suppose that it will be unfavourable to the revenue of India, because the Indian Government are so unfortunate as not to be able to increase their taxation.

1441. And the peculiarly unfavourable effect it will produce is this, that one considerable portion of the land revenue of India is either permanently or for a considerable period fixed in pecuniary amount, which amount is estimated in silver ?—Yes.

1442. Therefore, although from that circumstance inferences may come into operation to correct any bad effect which it may have on the trade of India, the loss which would arise to the revenue of India from that circumstance cannot be got over by any of the circumstances to which you have referred ?—I do not think there is any connection between the trade of India and the revenue of India for this purpose in the peculiar circumstances of the Indian Government, because they do not seem to be able to apply additional taxation.

1443. But as to the loss on the revenue, even if they could apply additional taxation, which is a fixed pecuniary amount, either fixed permanently or for a considerable number of years, there is no way of meeting that ?—No; that is a matter of agreement which cannot be altered.

Sir Charles Mills.

1444. You mentioned the demonetisation of silver by Germany

as being one of the causes. I suppose you will supplement that by the cessation of the demand for fresh coinage?—Quite so.

1445. It includes not only the selling of the silver, but also the cessation of the demand for fresh silver?—Yes.

1446. You stated that you thought it was very difficult to form any opinion as to the amount of silver and gold there was in circulation in the world? I think you go further, do you not, and say it is very difficult to form even an opinion as to the amount of gold in circulation in England?—There are very various estimates by very competent persons. Of course, it is much more possible to get near that than the circulation of the world, but such estimates are more matters of scientific conjecture than anything else.

1447. We had some figures given us as to the amount of thalers in Germany, do you think that those are also very doubtful?—Very dubious indeed. I have a strong belief that the Government do not themselves know; their whole policy is perplexed by uncertainty as to that, as far as an external observer can judge.

CHAIRMAN.

1448. When you speak of the drafts of the Government of India, you consider that those drafts, I presume, are determined by the amount that they require; it is not an open question how much money they can raise, or how much they need not raise?—I suppose that the drafts are regulated by the necessities of the Indian Government at home. They have a certain interest to pay, certain salaries to discharge, and certain things to buy, which are absolute necessities, I suppose.

1449. You do not wish to convey the idea, when you stated, as other witnesses have stated, that the increase in the drafts of the Indian Council are one of the causes which have led to the depreciation of silver, that it was at all a cause which the Indian Government could have avoided?—I apprehend it is not optional at all.

MR. FAWCETT.

1450. The great part of the expenditure of India is quite within the control of the Home Government here. I will give one illustration; for instance, so much had to be remitted from India to England for the payment for the buildings at the India Office. It was perfectly optional with the Government here whether they erected buildings. I do not mean to say whether they were wise in erecting the buildings they have, but it was optional for them to spend more or less, or the exact amount which they did spend on those buildings. Therefore the expenditure is within their control, but having sanctioned a certain expenditure, of course the amount they have to withdraw is not within their control?—Yes, it is only in that sense optional. Having determined their expenditure by political considerations, the money must come.

Made in the USA
Monee, IL
04 November 2026

67385022R00085